CW00970579

UFO
SPACE:1999

Chris Drake

ITC®
BOXTREE

First published in Great Britain in 1994 by
Boxtree Limited
Broadwall House
21 Broadwall
London SE1 9PL

10 9 8 7 6 5 4 3 2 1

Designed by Design 23, London
Printed and bound in the UK by Cambus Litho, East Kilbride, Glasgow

ISBN: 1 85283 393 9

A CIP catalogue entry for this book is available from the British Library

Acknowledgements
Thanks to the following for their advice, guidance and support:
Gerry Anderson, Graeme Bassett, Bob Bell, Ed Bishop, Mark Cady, Alan Gregory, Paul Hillam, Brian Johnson, John Keeble, Tony McKay, Sam Mitchell, Andrew Pixley, Roger Rice, Steve Robbins and Mitch Ross. Thanks especially to Krystyna Zukowska for inviting me to write the book and to Jake Lingwood for being an extremely helpful editor. Last, but by no means least, thanks to Mum and Dad for allowing me to use their dining room as an office – sorry for all the mess!

In addition to the above, I should like to give a special mention to Chris Bently, chairman of Fanderson – the official Gerry Anderson appreciation society – whose considerable assistance proved invaluable during the research and writing of this book. UFO and Space 1999, along with everything else Gerry has ever produced, are covered in great depth in the society's various magazines and video productions and anyone interested in joining should send an SAE to: Fanderson, PO Box 93, Wakefield, West Yorkshire, WF1 1JF.

CONTENTS

FOREWORD

When Boxtree asked me if I'd like to write a book on *UFO* and *Space:1999*, I didn't have to think too hard before saying yes. To be honest, I would almost have been prepared to pay them for the privilege because, to put none too fine a point on it, both *UFO* and *Space:1999* have been two of my favourite television programmes for as long as I can remember.

In the case of *UFO*, I would say that it *is* my all-time favourite and I can still remember exactly where I was when I first saw it, all those years ago.

In the early 1970s, as I recall, everyone believed that we were about to enter a marvellous new era of scientific achievement on space exploration. The Space Age, as it was known, never quite materialized, but to a young boy who dreamed of becoming an astronaut, *UFO* captured perfectly the feeling of excitement and optimism that was so prevalent at the time.

UFO had it all: a jet-fighter that could blast off out of the sea, secret headquarters underneath a film studio and mysterious green-skinned aliens who never revealed exactly what they were up to. Then, of course, there were the Moongirls, with their purple hair and silver mini-skirts. Why, I ask myself, can't they make programmes like this today?

By 1975 the Apollo missions had come to an end and the future of space travel looked decidedly bleak, but this didn't stop Gerry and Sylvia Anderson from unleashing their most spectacular and ambitious series onto an unsuspecting world. *Space:1999* rekindled that flame of early 1970's optimism which, albeit very briefly, burned a little brighter than anything this industry has managed to produce since.

Writing this book has been a great pleasure for me. Watching all the episodes again has brought back a flood of long-forgotten memories and, thanks to all the people who have helped me along the way, I've come out of it knowing a great deal more about both series.

Of all the programmes the Andersons ever produced (including *Thunderbirds* and *Captain Scarlet*), it is clear that *UFO* and *Space:1999* are studied more closely and by a greater number of people than any of the previous ones. It is to those thousands of devoted fans that this book is dedicated. It's been a long time coming. I hope you like it.

Chris Drake
November 25, 1993
Grimsby

Prologue

It was incredible. Like nothing he had ever seen before - and as a naval flyer, he thought he'd seen it all. But never anything like this. As he focused on the object through the viewfinder of his ciné camera, its strange irradiance lighting up the dark forest with an unnatural glow, Peter Carlin knew that he was looking at a spacecraft from another world.

'Peter, please.' Carlin heard his sister's voice and looked down into her terrified face; she had never expected anything like this when they had set off on the short drive into San Juan - just a few drinks to celebrate her brother's return home. Nothing could have prepared her for this. The fear in her voice was unmistakable, but Carlin knew that he couldn't tear himself away. Not yet. 'Take Jean back to the car,' he said, realizing that Leila's friend must be just as frightened as she was. 'I must get this.'

Then it happened. The sudden burst of machine-gun fire and Leila's friend was lifted off the ground and thrown back across the clearing by the force of the impact. 'Run!' shouted Carlin as his eyes were drawn involuntarily towards the bullet-ridden body. 'Run!'

More shots and, with the sound of his heart pounding in his ears, Carlin raced through the woods, trying desperately to draw their attacker away from his fleeing sister. Another burst of gunfire, closer now, and then a blinding pain in his left shoulder. Agonized, Carlin crashed to the ground; clutching at his shoulder he tried to rise, but the pain was too great and he fell back into the undergrowth.

As consciousness began to slip away, he thought he saw a figure, clad in a scarlet spacesuit, moving stealthily through the woods in the direction taken by his sister. Then, just before he passed out, Peter Carlin heard the unmistakable sound of a scream; a scream which froze the blood would haunt him day and night for the rest of his life.

◀ A spacecraft from another world – captured on film by Peter Carlin.

UFO

▲ From the depths of space – a UFO approaches the Earth.

Chapter 1

The Invasion is Planned

Somewhere in the Carina-Cygnus spiral arm of a galaxy called the Milky Way, there is a small, green and blue planet. Five thousand million people live on that planet and, at some point in their lives, there isn't a single one of them that hasn't looked up into the star-studded sky and wondered about the possibility of life somewhere else in the cosmos. In a distant part of the same galaxy, a dying race of infinitely superior beings located the small planet and saw, with some relief, that its inhabitants were very similar to themselves. Realizing that in these primitive, defenceless people they had found a slim chance of survival, they set out in their spacecraft to traverse the unimaginable void which separated their world from the little fertile planet known as Earth.

Invasion from space – the ultimate threat to mankind and the favourite theme of science fiction writers since the genre began. In the case of *UFO*, the format was the brain-child of Gerry and Sylvia Anderson, who, by 1969, had thrilled the world for almost a decade with such futuristic puppet adventures as *Fireball XL5*, *Stingray* and *Thunderbirds*. In 1967, the Andersons had explored the concept of an extraterrestrial threat, very successfully, with *Captain Scarlet and the Mysterons*. With its use of realistic, correctly proportioned puppets and often graphic depictions of violence, the programme moved away from the cozy, caricatured style that had been the trademark of Gerry's earlier shows and signalled the inevitable change over from puppets to people.

The Andersons' first fully fledged venture into the realm of live-action production was to be an extremely ambitious one – a spectacular and imaginative feature film entitled *Doppelganger*. The film starred American actor Roy Thinnes (best known for his role as David Vincent in Quinn Martin's *The Invaders*) and told of the discovery of a mirror-image Earth, orbiting the sun in perpetual opposition to our own planet. As well as containing what has to be the most realistic model rocket launch ever staged, the movie featured several actors who would later form the principal cast of *UFO*.

Although not a huge commercial success, *Doppelganger* opened to great critical acclaim and went a long way in proving Anderson's ability as a producer of live-action entertainment. Following the largely experimental and short-lived series *The Secret Service*, which featured an extensive mix of puppets and live-action ingredients, Gerry Anderson received the go ahead from Lew Grade, then the chairman of ATV, to embark upon his first full-scale live-action series. It was a move that Gerry had been aiming towards for several years and it clearly came as no great surprise to resident script editor Tony Barwick:

> *'I think that Gerry had taken puppets about as far as they could go and I really don't think he could do much more with them. He'd got them as realistic as possible, he'd mixed them with live-action; he'd done both television and feature films and so there really was nowhere else to go.'*

By early 1969, pre-production on the new series was at a well-advanced stage. With a reputation for producing small screen action as advanced as anything seen in the cinema, Gerry and Sylvia and their colleagues devised a format which provided every opportunity for spectacular model work and stunning futuristic locations of every kind.

▲ Norma Ronald and George Sewell – both had appeared in *Doppelganger* before joining the cast of *UFO* as Miss Ealand and Colonel Alec Freeman.

The year is 1985 and the Earth is under attack from a race of highly advanced aliens. Known only as UFOmen, these intruders have been visiting the planet for many years and, judging from the mutilated bodies that are often found after such visitations, it is clear that their intentions are hostile, even if their motives are unknown. Such are the capabilities of these alien marauders that an élite defence force known as UFoeDO (Unidentified Foe Defence Organization) is established and, operating from a huge security-tight building, Commander Edward Straker and his highly trained personnel fight back with all the awesome firepower at their disposal.

As the long and involved process of producing a television series got underway, so the original format underwent a number of very important changes. UFoeDO became SHADO – the new acronym standing for Supreme Headquarters Alien Defence Organization – and their earth-based headquarters was given a major change of location. Instead of the Pentagon-type building which was at first envisaged, the defence force would now be based in a secret headquarters situated beneath a fully functioning film studio! The new concept was not only more in keeping with the Andersons' preference for secret, carefully hidden organizations, but also a clever economy measure, as it meant that the ATV studios in Elstree, (not far from the MGM studios in Borehamwood, where the series was due to be filmed), could be utilized as an integral part of the concept; thus avoiding the need to build an expensive and elaborate model or travel far and wide in the search for a suitable location.

Meanwhile, at Century 21's special effects studio in Slough, the sophisticated hardware which would make up SHADO's impressive deterrent had to be designed and constructed. With Gerry and Sylvia Anderson busy supervising the development of the entire production, the actual design chores were handed over to a small team of experts, most of whom had worked with them since the very early days of *Supercar* and *Fireball XL5*.

Under the supervision of Derek Meddings, model designer Mike Trim realized the ideas for Moonbase and SID, SHADO'S sophisticated talking satellite; whilst Derek himself designed the submarine Skydiver, the tank-like SHADO Mobiles and the quite remarkable Moonbase Interceptors – complete with single, nose-mounted missile. It also fell upon Derek's shoulders to design and fly the amazing spinning UFOs which, for many people, were to become the stars of the show. As Derek has since revealed, the models appeared to rotate thanks to a spinning lower hull – to which paddle-shaped fins were attached – which revolved beneath a static perspex dome. Six wires were attached to the dome and it was from these that the model was suspended. When viewed on-screen, it really did look as though the entire UFO was spinning; the only disappointment was that they could not be made to bank, since, if the model was inclined at any angle other than the vertical, the motor caught and it immediately stopped going round!

As work on the model stages progressed, Art Director Bob Bell was busy designing the interior sets for all the various installations and vehicles. 'There was a very conscious projection of our imaginations into the future,' recalls Bob, looking back at the series today. 'Before the pilot film was made, Gerry had visited NASA and brought back plenty of reference material and photographs and those who designed the various craft, whether spacecraft or land vehicles, simply used their imaginations to carry these designs forward in time.' On the subject of his own designs, Bob is clear about the one which remains his favourite: 'When I watch episodes of the series today, I always feel a certain pleasure with Moonbase. It was designed simply as a circular set so that from most angles, the surface of the moon could be seen through the windows.'

Principle photography on the pilot episode, written by Gerry and Sylvia Anderson and entitled 'Identified', commenced in May 1969. By now, the series was firmly set in 1980 and American actor Ed Bishop had been cast in the role of SHADO's commander-in-chief, now known as Ed Straker. As well as appearing in the film *Doppelganger*, Bishop had worked with Gerry Anderson a couple of years earlier, when he had provided the voice of Captain Blue in *Captain Scarlet and the Mysterons*. Although a fine actor with a wealth of television and theatre work behind him, Bishop was not a well-known name in America, where a network sale would have resulted in considerable financial rewards. Gerry Anderson is quick, however, to defend his unusual casting decision.

'Making live-action science fiction is a terribly expensive business and, when I was casting for UFO, *I wanted to get somebody who was a good actor, who would turn up on time, who was very workmanlike and who understood British people – and that guy was Ed Bishop. I cannot say enough in support of that man; he is everything, I think, that an artist should be.'*

In the supporting role as Alec Freeman, Straker's second-in-command, was well-known British actor George Sewell. Like Bishop, Sewell had appeared in *Doppelganger* but, at the time, was probably better known for playing villains and 'heavies' of one sort or another. As Freeman, he was given the chance to play a more sympathetic character and show that he did, after all, have a kinder side to his nature. Besides Bishop and Sewell, the other key-roles within the series were filled by dancer Peter Gordeno as Skydiver Captain Peter Carlin and the beautiful Gabrielle Drake as the ice-cool Moonbase Commander, Lieutenant Gay Ellis.

The sets were superb, the costumes stunning

◀ Ed Straker's car approaches the Harlington Straker film studio – in reality, ATV's studios in Elstree.

◀ On one of the model stages in Slough, Derek Meddings supervises the filming of a finely detailed SHADO Mobile.

▼ An early design for the SHADO Mobile – drawn by Mike Trim.

and the special effects spectacular, but just three episodes into production it became clear that they were in trouble. Something was missing. Many of the episodes had been written to feature an Italian Moonbase Commander known as Franco Desica, but, for one reason or another, the character had never materialized and his role within the series had been taken, instead, by Lieutenant Ellis. As pre-production work began on 'Survival', an episode which would have seen Desica stranded on the surface of the moon, it became clear that what the series needed was a third male lead: a young hero who could fulfil the physical role that an action series required. Enter Paul Foster.

Played by 29-year-old Michael Billington, Paul Foster was an instant success and proved to be exactly what the series needed: a tough, slightly impetuous young man who enjoyed the excitement of his job and would clearly appeal to the female section of the audience. Following the filming of a special introductory story, which would explain Foster's absence during the first three episodes, the series progressed, with only minor changes within the cast until production was temporarily suspended in December 1969 due to the closure of the MGM studios.

Pinewood Studios in Buckinghamshire was chosen to be the new base of operations and plans were made to move the sets, props and cast to their new home as soon as possible. Unfortunately, suitable shooting stages would not be available until the following June so, during the interim, the production team moved back to their old studios in Slough (where most of the puppet shows had been made) and took the opportunity to assess the series and evaluate what had already been recorded on film.

When production recommenced in the early summer of 1970, several members of the cast, most notably George Sewell and Gabrielle Drake, had found employment elsewhere and it was realized that they would have to be replaced. On Moonbase, Lieutenant Nina Barry, played by Shirley Bassey lookalike Dolores Mantez, was promoted to the position of Moonbase

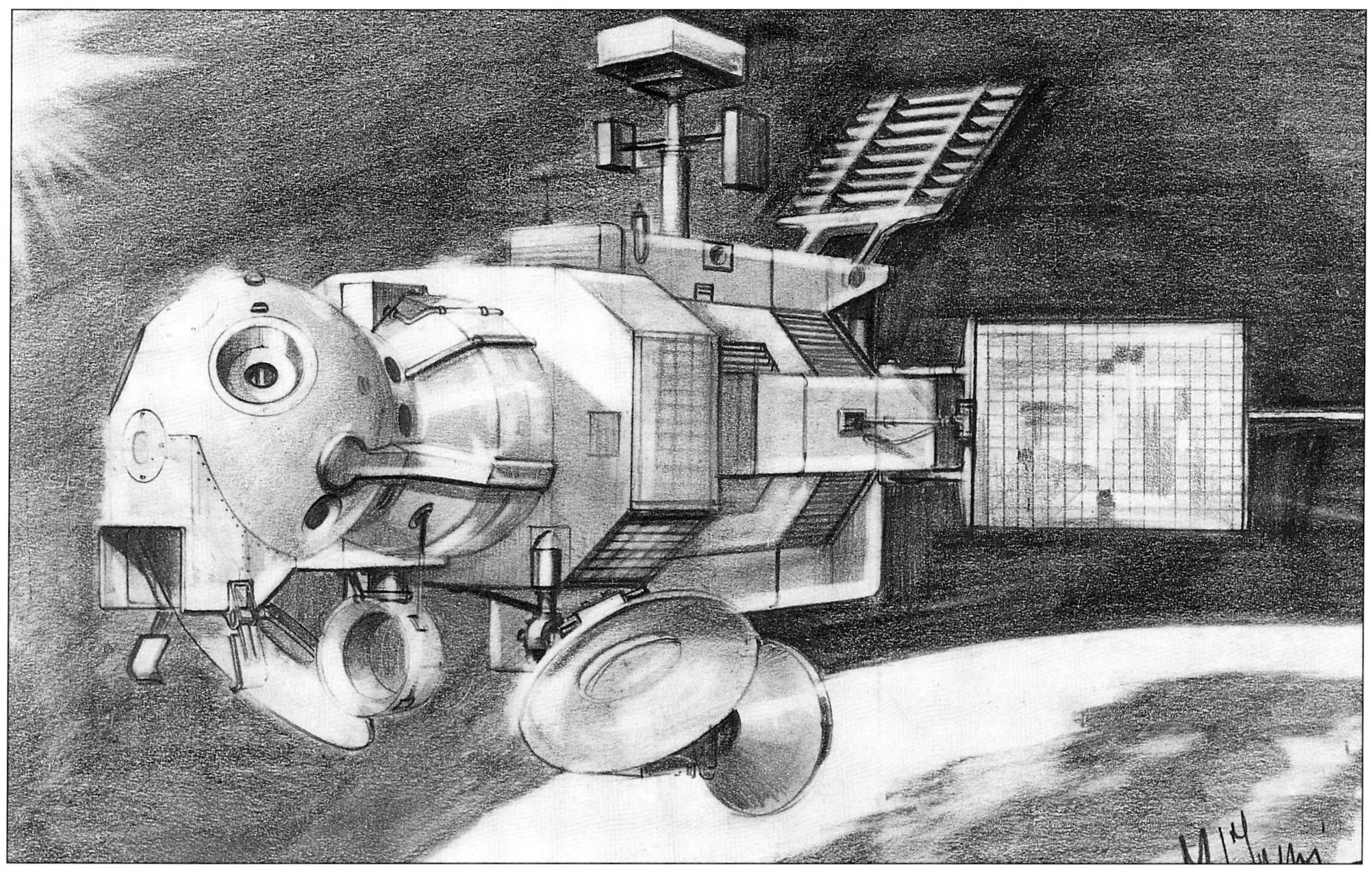

▲ Mike Trim's pre-production sketch of SID, the Space Intruder Detector.

◀ The enigmatic Commander Straker (Ed Bishop) receives some last minute attention from an ever-present make-up artist.

◀ The beautiful Wanda Ventham poses for a publicity shot with one of the futuristic SHADO cars.

Commander, whilst on Earth the vacancy at the top of SHADO proved a more difficult position to fill.

Having initially tried out a character known as Colonel John Grey, it was upon the suggestion of Ed Bishop that a minor character from the pilot episode – Virginia Lake, played by the elegant Wanda Ventham – should be reintroduced as Straker's second in command. As women were beginning to come to the fore in many professions around the world, this seemed like a good idea and, as from the episode 'The Cat With Ten Lives', Wanda Ventham became a addition to the cast.

On 16 September 1970, as filming proceeded on 'Timelash', the twenty-fourth episode to go into production, *UFO* began its nationwide run on British television. Unfortunately, a network sale had not been achieved and the show was broadcast by the various ITV stations at varying times and on different days of the week. Despite this, as the last of the 26 episodes went before the cameras, the series began to generate a very positive response and, encouraged by this reaction, the cast and crew completed their work with every expectation of resuming the following year. As things turned out, *UFO* would not run to a second series but would evolve, instead, into something completely different.

▼ Michael Billington, seen here in his command position on Moonbase, joined the cast of *UFO* in the episode 'Survival' and quickly became a firm favourite with female fans.

◀ An Alien. His helmet contains the life-sustaining green liquid necessary if he is to survive the prolonged journey to earth.

Chapter 2

The Intruders

'Who are they? Where do they come from? Why do they come?'

Three questions – three very important questions – posed by Ed Straker towards the end of the programme's first episode. But as the series develops, so it becomes clear that the more we learn about UFOs and their mysterious occupants, the less we really know.

Examination of the first Alien to fall into SHADO's hands reveals him to be humanoid – essentially, therefore, they are like us. Following the Alien's death – due, it seems, to a form of rapid ageing – a thorough postmortem reveals the full shocking truth: the Alien's heart, which is clearly a transplant, is undeniably human in origin. The revelation is enough to convince Straker that the Aliens are using the Earth as a form of glorified organ bank; flying in, often landing in remote, secluded areas and then simply taking what they need, quickly, quietly and without any remorse. The Aliens, it would seem, are driven by circumstance across the immeasurable gulf of space, spurred on by the strongest instinct in the universe – survival.

As to where they come from proves to be an altogether more difficult question to answer. 'Imagine a dying planet,' muses Straker, 'in some distant corner of the universe; its natural resources exhausted, its inhabitants sterile, doomed to extinction.' A grim prospect and certainly a situation from which anyone would be desperate to escape; but just how far are the Aliens prepared to travel in order to preserve their race?

One of the first things that is discovered upon examination of the captured Alien voyager is that his space helmet, and therefore his lungs, are filled with an oxygenated green liquid. Quite clearly, the liquid is intended to cushion the lungs and nasal cavity against the crushing effects produced by high-speed travel. The fact that the Alien's skin has obtained a green coloration from the liquid implies that, even at a velocity many times the speed of light, the Aliens have to travel for several months in order to reach the Earth. Their planet, therefore, must lie in the outer reaches of our galaxy, the Milky Way, if not beyond that.

So, what is the Alien planet like? The examined Alien has poorly developed muscles, which may indicate that his home planet has a relatively weak gravity compared to our own. Or, of course, his physical condition may have deteriorated simply as the result of his extended journey through space. However, the fact that upon the removal of his helmet, the Alien was able to breathe easily implies that the atmosphere on his world is very similar to our own – but with one important difference. After just a few hours' exposure, the Alien died from what appeared to be acute dehydration. It must be safe to assume, therefore, that whatever else may or may not be true, the Alien planet has an atmosphere which contains a far greater percentage of water than does our own.

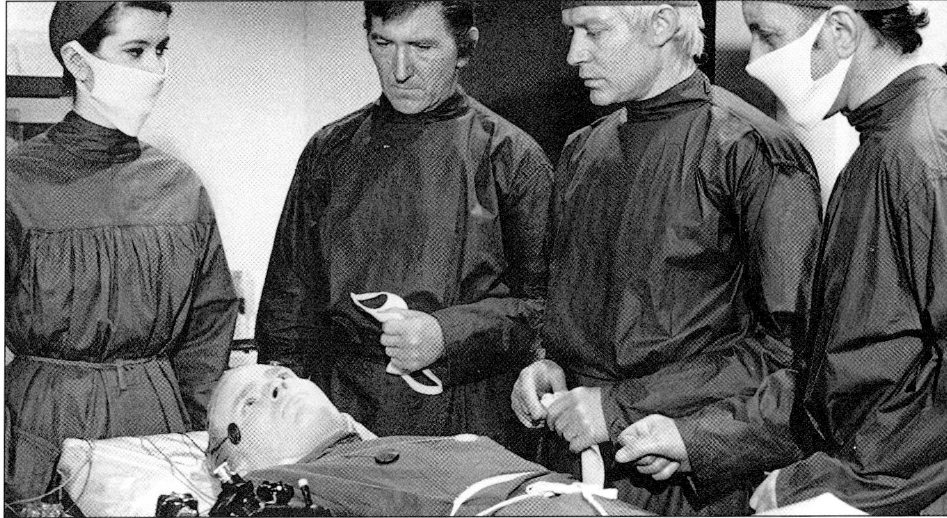

▲ In SHADO'S medical centre, Freeman, Straker and a team of surgeons examine a captured Alien. The results of their tests lead to a shocking discovery.

If, as seems to be the case, the Aliens must travel vast distances in their quest for replacement organs, some thought must be given to the means employed by them to propel their interplanetary craft. Because SHADO was never able to capture or examine any of these fantastic vehicles, theories regarding their construction and internal workings are, in the main, based purely upon conjecture and are therefore naturally open to debate.

One thing that is certain, however, is that they don't employ any conventional means of propulsion in order reach our planet; instead it seems quite likely that their drive units are based on some revolutionary form of force-field interaction, perhaps used in conjunction with a powerful charged-particle generator. Certainly in the episode 'Timelash', Straker speculates that the Aliens have used some sort of force-field in order to transcend the time barrier, whilst in 'Computer Affair', an incoming UFO collides with a speeding Interceptor and sustains only minor damage – a clear indication that it was protected in some way from the full force of the impact.

Another clue that points towards the force-field theory is the incredibly powerful destructive ray which, on several occasions, the UFOs are seen to unleash with devastating results. Whenever such a ray is fired, it always seems to emanate from a point on, or just off, the actual surface of the craft. It is more than likely, therefore, that this ray is in fact a fierce extension of the UFO's force-field which, having been supercharged, can be projected with great accuracy in any chosen direction.

▲ Following the destruction of a UFO, an Alien escape pod comes in to land, its occupant safe – for the time being . . .

If some of the Aliens' powers represent incredible advances in both science and technology, then others simply defy explanation. In the aforementioned 'Timelash', the Aliens succeed in freezing SHADO HQ in what can only be described as a *time bubble*. And in 'The Long Sleep', they are able to resurrect a dead hippy and extend his already unnatural lifespan still further by some means of genetic tampering. The process involved is far beyond anything even remotely possible in today's scientific climate, although it seems reasonable to assume that such an extended lifespan could only be achieved by removing certain coded information from the DNA structure of one individual and then implanting it into another.

It also becomes clear that the Aliens are able to harness, and in some way control, the ancient forces which, like an invisible thread, run through the very fabric of the universe. In the episode 'The Psychobombs', for instance, they take three perfectly normal people and alter them in such a way that they become living conduits – supernatural conductors, able to receive the latent energies which saturate the cosmos – and then ignite them with explosive results.

Unfortunately for the people on Earth, the human mind seems to be particularly susceptible to Alien conditioning and it is a weakness that they exploit on more than one occasion. In 'Kill Straker!', Paul Foster and a fellow astronaut are subjected to powerful brainwashing techniques that leave them with one objective – to kill their Supreme Commander! Whilst Craig Collins, in 'The Man Who Came Back' has the personality centres of his brain burned out and is returned to Earth as a form of radio-controlled assassin. However, perhaps the most interesting and revealing examples of Alien mind control can be seen in the episodes 'ESP' and 'The Cat With Ten Lives'.

In 'ESP', Straker and Freeman encounter John Croxley, a man tortured by his own inexplicable powers of advanced extrasensory perception. Able to foresee the future and read the thoughts of others, it eventually becomes clear that Croxley has some kind of incredible symbiotic link with the Aliens and that they have manipulated him until he is little more than an irrational, homicidal puppet. This episode is also

◀ Having removed his helmet, a stranded Alien takes refuge in a lonely house and uses a strange device to contact SHADO.

▼ Tormented by visions of the future, John Croxley (John Stratton) is unaware that his mind has been infiltrated by the Aliens and that he is nothing more than a pawn in their terrible inter-galactic game.

notable for the scene in which the usually mute Aliens, using Croxley as their mouthpiece, implore Straker to help them, revealing that their planet is indeed dying and insisting that they mean no harm to the people of Earth.

'The Cat With Ten Lives' is perhaps the ultimate story of this kind, as it deals not only with the paranormal aspects of mind control, but also gives a disturbing new twist to the previously accepted theories concerning the Aliens. When he is snatched and taken aboard a UFO, Interceptor pilot Jim Regan undergoes a radical form of conditioning which opens up a telepathic link between himself and a possessed Siamese cat. As if this isn't incredible enough, following his examination of an Alien body, Dr. Jackson discovers

▼ A grounded UFO fights back – unleashing a ray of incredible destructive power!

that the whole body, even the brain, is human in origin; leading him to speculate that the Aliens have no physical form at all, but are spiritual beings, living out their lives in stolen, brain-washed bodies,

Physical, spiritual, ethereal or otherwise, the Aliens of *UFO* remain as enigmatic today as they ever were. Their motives may have been questionable and their methods less than humane, but, in the final analysis, it is still difficult not to feel some kind of pity for them. Their powers are beyond comprehension and their knowledge as infinite as space itself, and yet, despite this, on a small planet in a distant part of the universe, their tragic race slides inexorably towards extinction.

▼ Having been given superhuman powers by the Aliens, Clem Mason (Mike Pratt) uses his amazing strength to break into a SHADO coastal installation.

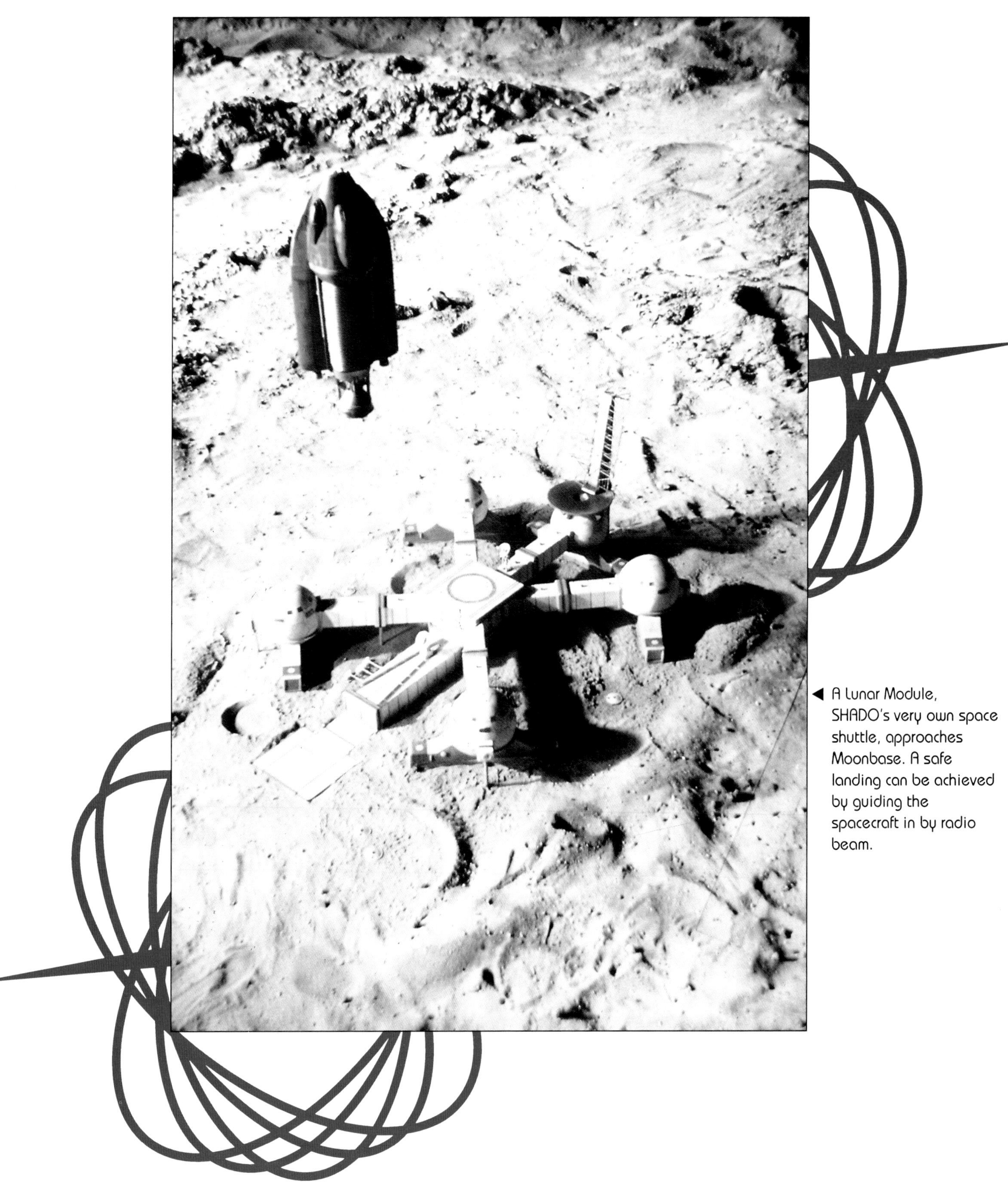

◀ A Lunar Module, SHADO's very own space shuttle, approaches Moonbase. A safe landing can be achieved by guiding the spacecraft in by radio beam.

Chapter 3

The Defenders

When in 1970 it became apparent that the visiting Aliens presented a very serious threat to mankind, the governments of the world united and, at considerable expense, a global defence force was set up. The organization was christened SHADO and equipped with every conceivable device and vehicle needed to combat the intelligent and highly advanced foe.

The total cost of equipping and running SHADO will probably never be known; the huge sums of money required come from secret black budgets which never appear on the balance sheets of the treasuries from which they originate, although it is safe to assume that the total amount must run into hundreds of billions of dollars. Similarly, the specialized hardware developed for and used by the organization is cloaked in secrecy and detailed information has proved difficult to obtain.

However, after painstaking research, it has been possible to build up a fairly clear picture of SHADO, its installations, personnel and equipment and this chapter represents the very first in-depth study of the world's most amazing and vital organization.

MOONBASE

Situated in the Sea of Tranquillity, the location of the first manned moon landing, Moonbase is the Earth's first line of defence against the Aliens. Consisting of five interconnected spheres and a number of below-surface facilities, Moonbase has a permanent crew of just fifty personnel, ranging from astronauts to technicians and command-level staff. During the late 1970s, whilst the base was being set up, it was discovered that women adapted better to the unchanging, rather sterile environment that the Moon offered and, as a result, it was decided that they should make up the majority of the installation's personnel.

◀ Space tracker Joan Harrington (Antonia Ellis) at her console in the Control sphere of Moonbase.

Of the five spheres (Control, Leisure, Sleep, Reactor and Reception), the Control sphere is, without doubt, the most important, as it is from here that incoming UFOs are monitored and all communication with Earth is carried out. From her centrally located control console, Moonbase commander Gay Ellis oversees the smooth running of the base and ensures that, with very few exceptions, even the most determined of Aliens is unable to reach the Earth.

One of the most intriguing features of Lieutenant Ellis and the other Moonbase girls has to be their bobs of metallic mauve hair. Far from being purely decorative, the wigs serve to protect the wearers from the migraine-inducing electromagnetic fields which, unfortunately, are produced by the powerful Control sphere equipment.

THE INTERCEPTORS

Housed in an airtight launch bay, below the lunar surface, the three Moonbase Interceptors are on constant standby, armed and ready to meet the dangerous intruders head-on.

When a UFO is detected, usually on the outer limits of the solar system, the alarms go off and the order is given for immediate launch. Standing by in the Leisure sphere, the three on-duty pilots grab their helmets and leap into the special chutes which deliver them in a matter of seconds to the launch bay and their waiting craft. As soon as the support crews are clear, the air is pumped out of the bay and the Interceptors are elevated on hydraulic platforms to their launch positions, which are disguised as craters on the lunar surface above.

Once spaceborne, the Interceptors, which are driven by nuclear rockets, are guided by Moonbase until they are directly within the flight path of the incoming UFO. Having received details of the UFO's range, speed and trajectory, the Interceptors fire their single nuclear missiles which, thanks to sophisticated proximity fuses, can be programmed to explode as soon as they reach the predicted vicinity of the Alien craft. Due to the unlikelihood of actually hitting a speeding UFO, this method of interception was considered to be the most effective as the need for a direct hit was eliminated. All that was required was for the UFO to fly into the explosion or be caught by the tremendous shockwave and it would be destroyed, or so badly damaged as to make it an easy target should it enter the Earth's atmosphere.

SPACE INTRUDER DETECTOR

Orbiting the Earth at a distance of 36,000 kilometres, the Space Intruder Detector (or SID for short) is SHADO's purpose-built early warning system. Containing the most powerful computer known to man, SID is capable of detecting and tracking incoming UFOs even at extreme range and, thanks to a revolutionary speech circuit, is able to provide Moonbase and SHADO headquarters with a verbal commentary on any situation as it develops. A vital link in Earth's defence system, SID's importance cannot be overstated and it must be considered a prime target for Alien attack.

SKYDIVER

Like a bizarre cross between fighter aircraft and nuclear submarine, Skydiver prowls the ocean depths, ready to strike at any intruder able to bypass the outer defences and enter its operational range.

Constructed out of HY130 (an incredibly strong form of high-yield steel), the submarine section of Skydiver can operate safely at a depth of 620 fathoms, although a maximum depth of 750 fathoms has been achieved before serious structural damage forced the vessel to level off. With a maximum submerged speed of 40 knots, Skydiver is propelled by reactor-driven steam

▶ **Above, left:** *'Interceptors immediate launch!'* On permanent stand-by in the Leisure sphere, the Interceptor pilots react to an alert by leaping into the special chutes which will take them to their waiting craft.

◀ On the lunar surface, the three Moonbase interceptors are raised to their launch positions on hydraulic platforms.

▲ Skydiver, flagship of SHADO's submarine fleet, cruises the oceans of the world – ready to engage any UFO which manages to slip past the outer defences.

▶ In geo-stationary orbit high above the Earth, SHADO's Space Intruder Detector (SID) maintains a constant watch for approaching UFOs.

turbines, enclosed within vented-tubes on either side of its hull.. This arrangement (that is, water sucked into the tubes through forward intakes) reduces the wake produced, making the submarine almost impossible to detect with even the most sophisticated equipment. During surface patrols, much greater speed can be achieved by lowering hydroplanes, thus raising the bow of the craft clear of the water and allowing it to skim the ocean like a catamaran.

Piloted by Skydiver's Captain, Sky One is launched from the submarine at an angle of 45 degrees, and blasts itself out of the water with powerful twin rockets, before switching over to conventional jet engines when correct altitude and airspeed have been achieved. Capable of travelling at Mach 2 (twice the speed of sound), Sky One is armed with 40 SkySting missiles, which are programmed to detonate in mid-flight if they miss their projected target.

Clearly a formidable weapon, an unspecified number of these amazing craft are known to exist and extensive research suggests that they were built by the Electric Boat Division of the General Dynamics Corporation. Between 1971 and 1976, a mysterious gap appears in the building programme of the Los Angeles Class submarine and, as General Dynamics are also responsible for designing and constructing the F111 and F16 fighter aircraft, the conclusion is inevitable, although impossible to prove.

Skydiver, the flagship of the fleet, is currently

▶
Following the landing of a UFO, three SHADO Mobiles converge on the grounded intruder.

captained by Lew Waterman, a former Interceptor pilot. He replaced the vessel's first captain, Peter Carlin, who is known to have been killed in action during a particularly dangerous UFO incident.

THE MOBILES

Concealed in secure depots throughout the world, the SHADO Mobiles serve as armoured personnel carriers, capable of transporting both men and equipment to the scene of a grounded UFO. Fitted with heavy-duty caterpillar tracks, the vehicles are able to traverse even the most rugged terrain with ease and, although not heavily armed, their turret-mounted machine guns are powerful enough to bring down an escaping UFO. Built by an unknown manufacturer to SHADO specifications, the Mobiles operate in groups of three and are often carried to their required location by SHADO aircraft or unobtrusive articulated lorries.

▶
Having blasted off from Diver 1, Sky 1 is seen above the clouds, racing to intercept an approaching UFO.

▶
Peter Carlin, a former naval pilot, captained Skydiver until his tragic death in a particularly nasty UFO incident. Carlin was played by Peter Gordino.

SHADO HEADQUARTERS, EARTH.

Forty miles due west of London, in the area commonly known as Wessex, lies the industrial town of Harlington. Amongst other things, Harlington is the home of one of England's oldest and most successful film studios. Once described by Alexander Korda as 'the finest film studio this side of Hollywood', it was here, in 1938, that the great producer made his spectacular version of H.G. Wells' *The War of the Worlds*. Forty-two years later, the studio is once again in business but, unknown to the 400 people who work there, a very real intergalactic war is planned and co-ordinated from beneath their very feet.

When SHADO was being set up, it was decided that total secrecy should be maintained. No one amongst the general public must know about the organization or its awesome purpose; quite apart from the unfriendly military powers who might use its advanced technology to their advantage, knowledge of the Alien threat would only cause mass hysteria throughout the world as the population at large realize that they are not safe at night, even in their own homes. For this reason, a secret location for SHADO's Earth-based headquarters had to be found – and that location turned out to be an abandoned film studio in the area of Great Britain most frequently troubled by UFO activity.

Having been purchased by the British government, the original plan was to demolish the studio buildings and redevelop the entire site as an industrial estate. However, realizing that a fully functioning film studio would provide his organization with the perfect cover, Ed Straker saw to it that long before SHADO headquarters became operational, the Harlington-Straker Film Studios were open for business.

With laboratories, medical centre, conference room, firing range and even a restaurant, SHADO headquarters is a maze of reinforced corridors and tunnels, entered by way of carefully disguised elevators and concealed stairwells. Ed Straker and SHADO's command personnel prefer to use the executive elevator which, situated in

▶ Usually found in SHADO Control, senior operative Lt. Johnson, played by Ayshea Brough, works above ground, maintaining her 'cover'as a busy studio P.A.

the studio's modern administration block, doubles as Straker's studio office. After he has entered the office, the doors are firmly locked and, having identified himself to a desk-top voice print analyser, Straker flicks a switch and watches as the entire room is lowered eighty feet to the headquarters below. The nerve centre of SHADO headquarters is the lead-lined control room, situated at the very heart of the complex. Like a fortified bunker, the control room contains the banks of computers, communications and monitoring equipment necessary to co-ordinate the efforts of SHADO's worldwide network of outposts and defence installations.

Adjacent to the control room is Straker's ultra-modern SHADO office. Equipped with, amongst other things, a direct video-link to Moonbase, it is from here that Straker makes many of the life or death decisions which affect not only the personnel of SHADO but the people of planet Earth.

In his underground office, Commander Straker discusses tactics with Colonel Freeman.

An International Band of Heroes

▲ Ignoring the risks involved, Straker is often quick to leave the comparative safety of SHADO HQ and take an active role in even the most dangerous of operations. Here he is seen alongside LT. Nina Barry (Dolores Mantez) aboard the SHADO submarine Skydiver.

COMMANDER ED STRAKER

Described by General Henderson as SHADO's most vital piece of hardware, there can be no doubt that when it comes to the defence of Earth, Commander Edward Straker is just as important as Skydiver, the Interceptors or SID.

Born in Boston on 10 July 1940, Straker excelled at school, particularly in science-based subjects and with dreams of becoming an astronaut, he graduated from Yale with a degree in astrophysics, before doing two years lunar research at the Massachusetts Institute of Technology. Joining the United States Airforce in the early 1960s, Straker test-flew a number of experimental jet aircraft before being accepted on to NASA's astronaut training programme in 1964 Heavily involved in the Gemini programme, he was held in reserve for the Gemini 12 mission of November 1966 and only active service in Vietnam prevented him from being aboard Apollo 7 when it orbited the Earth 163 times in October 1968.

Having observed a number of unidentified objects whilst flying in the war zone, Straker's interest in the phenomena was fired and, upon his return to the United States, he joined Project Blue Book and became deeply involved in the investigation of reported UFO incidents. Having obtained conclusive proof that UFOs were indeed visiting the Earth, Straker set out to alert the governments of the world about the Alien threat. Arriving in England, the car that was to take him to Chequers and a meeting with the British prime minister was attacked by one of the very craft he had set out to expose. Although the valuable evidence was destroyed, the incident validated Straker's story beyond all possible doubt and spurred the world's authorities into taking immediate and decisive action.

A massive pooling of resources resulted in the formation of SHADO, and Straker, with his impressive track-record and total dedication to duty, was quickly and unanimously voted in as the organization's commander-in-chief.

COLONEL ALEC FREEMAN

If Straker comes across as a rather cold strategist, then Alec Edward Freeman represents the warmer, more humane face of SHADO.

Born on 31 August, 1938 in Islington, north London, Freeman overcame a childhood blighted by illness to join the RAF, rising to the position of squadron leader before joining DS8, the RAF secretariat which, in the late 1960s, was responsible for investigating internal reports of unidentified flying objects. It was while he was with DS8 that Freeman first came into contact with Ed Straker and, having impressed the young American, he soon became SHADO's first recruit.

As Straker's closest friend, Freeman acted

▶ A popular member of SHADO, Alec Freeman is not only Straker's second-in-command but also his closest friend.

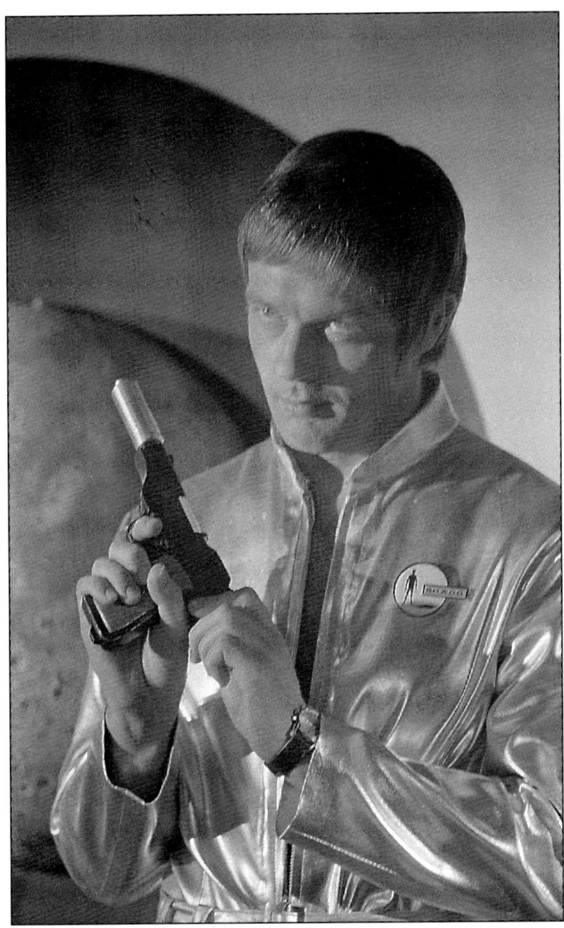

◀ Paul Foster, SHADO's resident man-of-action. When the going gets tough, Foster gets going – and somebody usually gets it in the neck.

as best man at his wedding and was on hand to offer support and advice when, due to the pressures of his work, the marriage ran into trouble less than a year later. In the episode 'Confetti Check A-OK' he is horrified to learn that Straker is planning to tell Mary about SHADO in an attempt to make her understand her better. He is able to convince Straker that he would be making a terrible mistake and that such knowledge would put both the organization and his wife in great danger.

Something of a humanitarian, Freeman doesn't always agree with Straker's methods and is particularly critical of his reliance upon computers. Despite personal differences, however, it is clear that he has a high regard for Straker, not only in a professional capacity but also as a friend, and his loyalty and support are never in question.

No on-screen reason is ever given for Freeman's disappearance after 17episodes, but it is safe to assume that, possibly upon Straker's personal recommendation, he accepted further promotion and went on to command a smaller SHADO base in some other part of the world.

COLONEL PAUL FOSTER

Paul Joseph Foster is a man who likes to live on the edge. Whether commanding Moonbase or leading the assault on a grounded UFO, Foster displays a clear disregard for his own safety and performs at his best when in the line of fire.

Born on 25 November 1951 in Knutsford, Cheshire, Foster gained a degree in physics from London University before joining the RAF at the age of 22. It was whilst he was in the RAF that he first encountered the phenomena of UFOs, reporting strange unidentified objects first in March 1974, then again in September 1977.

Searching constantly for a new challenge, Foster left the RAF in 1978 to become a test pilot with the Ventura Aircraft Corporation. It was while he was test-flying the XV-104 fighter-bomber that he and his co-pilot witnessed the destruction of an incoming UFO by Sky One. Caught in the blast, the aircraft was destroyed and Foster's co-pilot killed. Paul narrowly escaped and risked his career by sticking to his incredible story. Ed Straker was so impressed by the brash young man that he invited him to join SHADO. It was an offer that Paul Foster accepted without hesitation.

Having excelled in all areas during his rigorous training programme, Foster is quickly promoted to the rank of colonel and given command of SHADO's lunar installation, Moonbase. As Moonbase commander, his place is in the Control sphere but such is his nature that at the first sign of trouble he prefers to leave the relative safety of the base and involve himself directly with the action. Like everyone else in SHADO, Foster is ostensibly employed by Straker International, so that he may enter and leave the studios without arousing suspicion. In Foster's case, his 'cover' is that of production supervisor, a job which he clearly relishes, to the extent that he can often be found on the studio floor or in one of the preview theatres watching reel after reel of 'rushes'.

LIEUTENANT GAY ELLIS

Born in Thaxted, Essex, Moonbase commander Gay Ellis was educated at Roedean School for Girls, before studying pure mathematics at Cambridge University. She graduated with a

▶
Gay Ellis (Gabrielle Drake); cool and efficient – the perfect woman to take command of Moonbase.

first class honours degree then surprised her parents by entering the Womens Royal Army Corp., explaining that a career in accountancy or banking was not what she had in mind. Her leadership qualities soon came to the fore and in 1979 she was approached by SHADO and willingly accepted the challenge of a lunar posting.

As cool as she is attractive, Gay has no difficulty in maintaining a clear head during even the most abnormal of situations and her calm, clipped voice is both reassuring and authoritative.

Although undeniably well liked, she tends to keep herself very much to herself, doubtless aware that her position of authority naturally precludes her from entering into a relationship with any of her subordinates. On the one occasion that she breaks this rule, her involvement with Interceptor pilot Mark Bradley causes them both a certain degree of personal trouble and from then on, she projects a definite aura of unapproachability which even Paul Foster is unable to penetrate.

Clearly aware of her unique position in SHADO she is, on occasion, prone to work twice as hard as her male colleagues as if she has some kind of point to prove – a fact which does not go unnoticed by Commander Straker. Naturally outranked by Colonel Foster, Gay seems slightly put out when he is given temporary command of Moonbase during his early days in SHADO and she appears to be happier when he is not around. Their relationship whilst he is on the base is clearly a formal one.

No reason is ever given for the Lieutenant's departure from her position of command but, considering the personal restrictions imposed by close confinement on the Moon, it seems reasonable to assume that she applied for a more permissive Earth-based posting.

▶
Don't be fooled by those baby blue eyes; Colonel Virginia Lake is more than a match for anything the Aliens can throw at her.

COLONEL VIRGINIA LAKE

Glamorous, ambitious and highly intelligent, Virginia Carol Lake first encountered SHADO as a civilian designer, but went on to join the organization and ended up in a position of power second only to that of

▼ The dusky Lt. Nina Barry; she and Commander Straker go back a long way, but the true extent of their friendship is known only to themselves.

Commander Straker.

Born in Swansea in 1946, Virginia gained a degree in computing and mathematics from Bristol University before going on to do postgraduate research in utronic wave formation at Harvard University. Her work brought her to the attention of NASA and, in 1973, she was recruited to take charge of their Star Search space investigation programme. In 1978, having made several significant advances in her chosen field, Virginia left NASA to join Westbrook Electronics, SHADO's commercially run research and development facility. It was during her time at Westbrook that Virginia designed and perfected the advanced equipment which would allow SHADO to track the incoming UFOs that had managed to evade conventional means of detection for so long.

When it became clear that she would be spending a great deal of time on Moonbase in order to supervise the installation and operation of the utronic equipment, Virginia was formerly recruited into SHADO and given temporary command of the outpost following the departure of Lieutenant. Ellis. Straker was quick to recognize the woman's considerable decision-making and leadership skills and, when Alec Freeman's position as second-in-command became vacant, Virginia was offered the job – an offer she was to accept without hesitation.

LIEUTENANT NINA BARRY

Of all the high-ranking women within SHADO, the beautiful Nina Barry could be said to exude the most warmth and charm.. Her casual manner and cat-like grace make her one of SHADO's most popular and attractive personnel and it comes as no great surprise to learn that she was, through no fault of her own, largely responsible for the break-up of Ed Straker's marriage.

Born in Trinidad, the daughter of a Royal Navy officer, Nina came to England with her parents at an early age and, following a reasonably successful education, she joined the Womens Royal Naval Service (better known as the Wrens), where she served as a radar and communications operator at a number of important coastal installations. In 1970, upon the recommendation of her commanding officer, she was recruited by SHADO and played an active role in the setting-up of the fledgling organization. Her role in the break-up of Straker's marriage was an entirely accidental one when, having been photographed together by a private detective, Straker had no choice but to let his suspicious wife believe the obvious, rather than

reveal the true identity of his beautiful young companion.

By the late 1970s, due to her naval background, Nina was training for duty aboard Skydiver, the flagship of SHADO's impressive submarine fleet. Despite her excellence beneath the waves, Nina surprised her colleagues by requesting a lunar posting, where, after less than a year, she would rise to the position of Moonbase commander.

GENERAL JAMES HENDERSON

Apart from the Aliens, it often seems that the antagonistic General Henderson is Ed Straker's most dedicated foe.

Formerly with the Air Force Office of Special Investigations, Henderson had been seriously injured when the car in which he and Straker had been travelling was attacked by a UFO shortly after their arrival in England. Although he was to make a full recovery, his injuries

▲ The volatile General James Henderson (Grant Taylor); a man responsible for giving Straker more than the occasional ear-bashing.

prevented him from taking an active role in the discussions which resulted in the formation of SHADO. Having initially been tipped to head the proposed organization, Henderson could do little but sit back and watch as Straker was elevated to the position he had hoped would automatically be his.

When the world governments decided to set up SHADO, they also established a global agency known as the International Astrophysical Commission. Officially the Commission would regulate and authorize all aspects of space and lunar activity; unofficially they would keep an eye on SHADO, providing it with the money it required to maintain its many vehicles, spacecraft and installations. Following his complete recovery, Henderson quickly became chairman of the Commission, a job many people believe he attained thanks to his numerous friends in high places.

Now, from his position of power within the IAC's London building, Henderson clearly enjoys making life difficult for Straker and misses no opportunity to discredit the commander or remind him that it is he who is holding the purse strings.

DOCTOR DOUG JACKSON

The enigmatic Dr Jackson is SHADO's very own man of mystery. Despite his extremely English sounding name, his east European accent indicates that it is certainly a pseudonym, most probably adopted, in order to cover his tracks. Very little is known of his background prior to his joining SHADO, although some believe that he defected from Russia sometime in the 1960s, bringing with him a wealth of knowledge accumulated during his time in their secret service.

His movements during the 1970s are not well documented, although it is almost certain that he was connected with the British secret service in some way, and a character answering his description is reported to have been present at the debriefing of several Russian defectors and spies. It is not until 1979 that a clear record of his employment begins when, in August of that year, he joins the International Astrophysical Commission as security advisor and psychoanalytic consultant to SHADO.

As events proceed, so Jackson is seen to become an integral part of the organization, basing himself in a small office-cum-laboratory within the headquarters' psychoanalytic unit and coming up with some of the more outlandish theories regarding the Aliens and their amazing powers. With his quiet, deliberate mode of speech and slightly sinister manner, Jackson is never the most popular member of SHADO; in fact he is openly disliked by many, including Alec Freeman. Despite this, his value to the organization cannot be overstated and he is, without doubt, the most intriguing human character to appear in any episode of the series.

▼ The late Vladek Sheybal played Doctor Doug Jackson, a mysterious but essential member of SHADO's personnel.

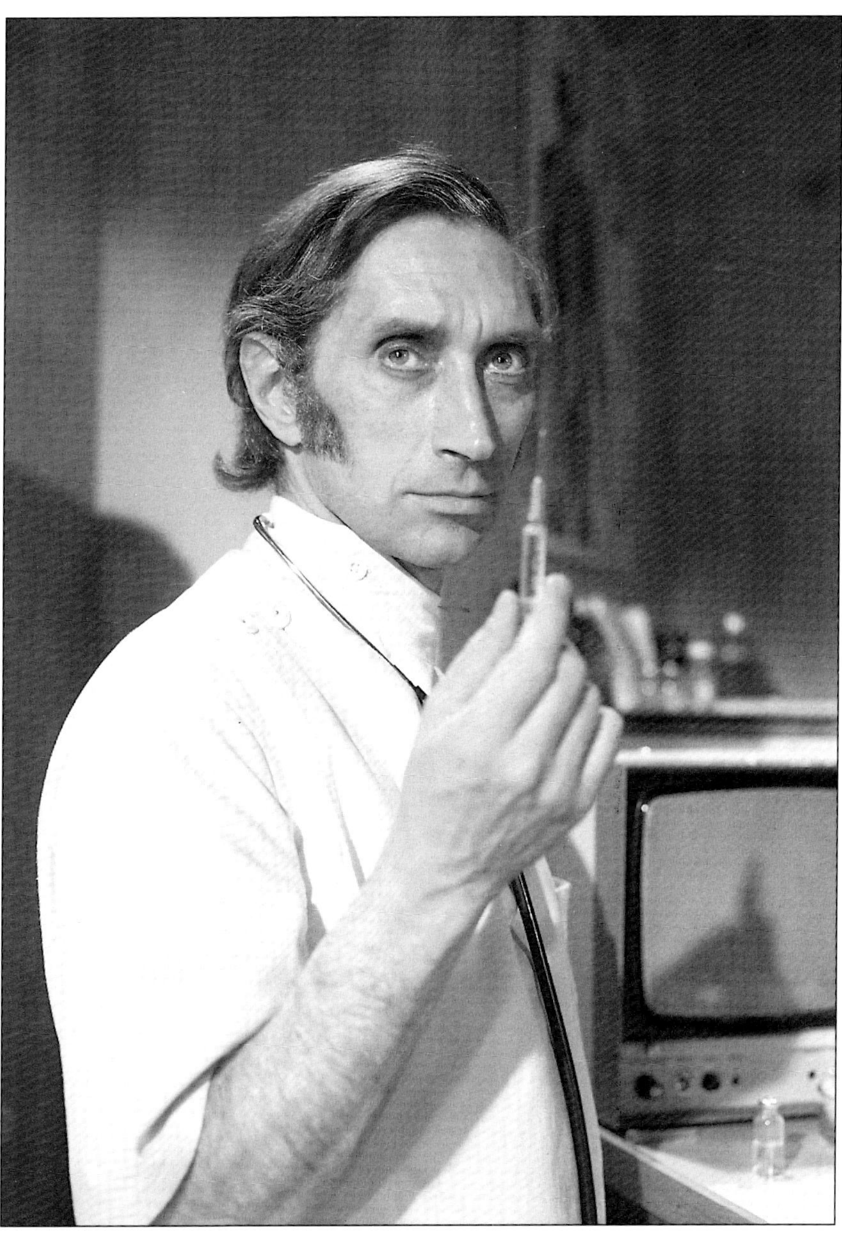

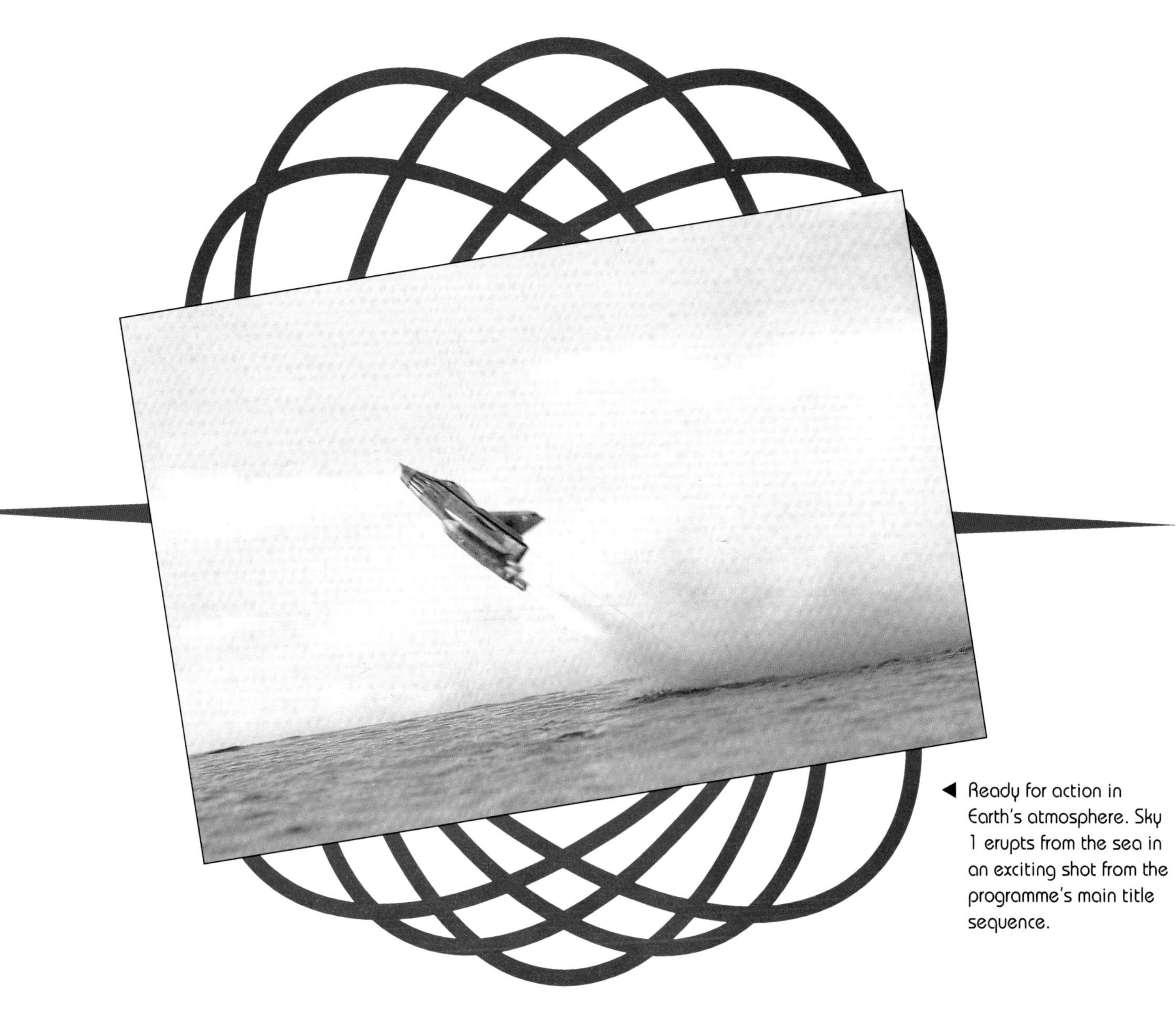

◀ Ready for action in Earth's atmosphere. Sky 1 erupts from the sea in an exciting shot from the programme's main title sequence.

Chapter 4

Sighting Confirmed

SHADO's fight against the Aliens was to last for a total of 26 episodes, each with an approximate running-time of 50 minutes.

Each episode begins with the impressive opening-title sequence, a tightly edited montage of shots which introduces the viewer to SHADO, its key installations and vehicles and the principal cast. Explanatory information is provided courtesy of a teleprinter, whilst the captions 'UFO', 'SHADO' and '1980' are flashed up at regular intervals at almost subliminal speed. The sequence is given added momentum by Barry Gray's memorable theme, an up-tempo piece, arranged for brass, Hammond organ and electric guitar which captures perfectly the exciting and dramatic mood of the series.

Following a short prologue, which would set the scene and hopefully hook the viewers, the picture would freeze and the letters 'UFO' would bleed in from different angles, filling the screen with the distinctive series logo. The principal cast and production team would then be credited over the opening shots of the first act or, in the case of 'Reflections in the Water', over a montage of clips from the following episode.

The closing credits were displayed over a simple but effective shot of the Sun, Moon and Earth seen against the infinite and starry backdrop of space. The camera pulls back until, quite unexpectedly, what appears to be the Alien planet looms into view. Backed with a haunting electronic theme, the sequence manages to convey something of the ethereal nature of the series and is strangely disconcerting.

This chapter covers all 26 episodes of the series, complete with plot synopses and writer/director and guest cast credits. The episodes are presented in production order, with the exception of 'Survival' and 'Exposed' which, for reasons of continuity, have been transposed.

IDENTIFIED

Teleplay by **Gerry and Sylvia Anderson** with **Tony Barwick**
Directed by **Gerry Anderson**

Ten years after almost losing his life in a UFO incident, former airforce Colonel Ed Straker sits at the helm of SHADO – a top secret organisation dedicated to the defence of Earth against the Alien aggressor. When a new tracking system is developed which will allow SHADO to detect the UFOs even in deep space, Colonel Alec Freeman is sent to Los Angeles to oversee the transportation of the equipment and its design team. The Aliens, however, are one step ahead and, as the SHADO aircraft crosses the Atlantic, a UFO eludes the Moonbase defences and moves in for the kill.

Guest stars

Cabinet Minister	**Basil Dignam**
Kurt Mahler	**Paul Gillard**
Phil Wade	**Gary Files**
Ken Matthews	**Michael Mundell**

▼ When a UFO crash-lands in Canada, Gay Ellis and Alec Freeman co-ordinate the search operation, directing the three SHADO Mobiles on to their target. (Computer Affair)

COMPUTER AFFAIR

Teleplay by **Tony Barwick**
Directed by **David Lane**

When an Interceptor is destroyed by an incoming UFO, the computers indicate human error. Could an emotional attachment between Moonbase controller Gay Ellis and one of her subordinates have influenced a crucial life or death decision? Straker is convinced, but Freeman has enough doubt in his mind to want to prove him wrong. When the damaged UFO is located in Canada, Freeman sets out to bring in the crew – taking with him Lieutenant Ellis and Interceptor pilot Mark Bradley in the hope that their actions in the field will justify the faith he has in them.

Guest stars

Dr. Murray	**Peter Burton**
Ken Matthews	**Michael Mundell**

FLIGHT PATH

Teleplay **Ian Scott Stewart**
Directed by **Ken Turner**

Moonbase operative Paul Roper has been 'got at' by the Aliens. In order to protect his wife, Roper uses SID to compute a flight path which can be followed by a UFO in order to attack Moonbase. Having caught Roper passing on the information, Straker and Freeman are faced with the puzzle of how to intercept the UFO, which will almost certainly be making the attack under cover of heavy sunspot activity. Determined to make amends, Roper volunteers to take a rocket launcher out onto the lunar surface and wait for the UFO to appear.

Guest stars

Paul Roper	**George Cole**
Carol Roper	**Sonia Fox**

▼ Aboard an experimental aircraft, Paul Foster and his co-pilot (Matt Zimmerman) refuse to leave the area when they make visual contact with an in-coming UFO. (Exposed)

▲ Friend or foe? Stranded on the Moon, Paul Foster comes face to face with an Alien. (Survival)

EXPOSED

Teleplay **Tony Barwick**
Directed by **Dave Lane**

Test pilot Paul Foster refuses to keep his mouth shut when his aircraft is destroyed by an exploding UFO. His co-pilot died in the ensuing crash and he knows what he saw. His boss warns him against pursuing the matter and Jackson, posing as a military investigator, treats the whole thing as a joke – but Foster isn't laughing. And neither is Ed Straker when Foster arrives at the film studio and threatens to expose him and whatever it is he is hiding. Realizing that his impetuous visitor means business, Straker reveals that the whole thing has been an elaborate test and that Foster has passed with flying colours.

Guest stars

Janna Wade	**Jean Marsh**
William Kofax	**Robin Bailey**
Jim Wade	**Matt Zimmerman**
Louis Graham	**Arthur Cox**

SURVIVAL

Teleplay **Tony Barwick**
Directed by **Alan Perry**

Foster's position as Moonbase commander almost comes to a premature end when an Alien, having managed to land undetected on the Moon, succeeds in shooting out a porthole in the Leisure sphere. Foster escapes with his life, but the explosive decompression kills Bill Grant – an astronaut nearing the end of his tour of duty. Seeking revenge for his friend's death, Foster leads an expedition onto the lunar surface to locate the Alien sniper. When the grounded UFO opens fire on the astronauts, Straker orders its destruction and Foster is believed to have perished in the explosion. Injured and with his radio knocked out, Foster struggles to make it back to Moonbase. It is then that he comes face to face with the similarly stranded Alien.

Guest stars

Tina Duval	**Suzan Farmer**
Bill Grant	**Robert Swann**
Alien	**Gito Santana**

▲ Following a serious car accident, Straker joins his ex-wife (Suzanne Neve) and her new husband (Philip Madoc) as they receive news of their injured son's condition. (A Question of Priorities)

CONFLICT

Teleplay **Ruric Powell**
Directed by **Ken Turner**

Space junk can be extremely dangerous – especially if an Alien satellite is using it as cover to ambush SHADO spacecraft! When Straker insists that the International Astrophysical Commission carries out a total-clearance programme, General Henderson laughs in his face; the cost would be staggering and, without a good reason, he will authorize nothing. Straker is at a loss until Foster takes the law into his own hands and, breaking the lunar flight embargo, lures the Alien device out into the open and gets the proof his commander so desperately needs.

Guest stars

Captain Steve Maddox	**Drewe Henley**
Crewman – lunar module	**David Courtland**
Steiner	**Michael Kilgarriff**

THE DALOTEK AFFAIR

Teleplay **Ruric Powell**
Directed by **Alan Perry**

Paul Foster is convinced that a nearby mining installation is responsible for the communication blackouts which have isolated Moonbase and caused an incoming Lunar Module to crash. Despite protests from the Dalotek team, he removes vital components from their powerful geo-scanner, believing it to be the cause of the problems. When another blackout plays havoc with their tracking systems, Moonbase is left blind to the approach of a UFO. It is then that the Dalotek team discover a strange device nestling in a deep crater. Realizing that this must be the true source of the interference, Foster dispatches a Moon Mobile to blow it up. But can they reach it before the UFO reaches them?

Guest stars

Jane Carson	**Tracy Read**
Mark Tanner	**Clinton Greyn**
Phil Mitchell	**David Weston**
Dr Frank E. Stranges	**Himself**

A QUESTION OF PRIORITIES

Teleplay **Tony Barwick**
Directed by **David Lane**

Straker's life becomes even more complicated when John, his young son, is knocked down by a speeding car and is seriously injured. Informed by a doctor that only a special anti-allergenic drug can save the boy's life, Straker arranges for a SHADO aircraft to pick the drug up from New York and fly it quickly to England. Unaware of Straker's motives, Freeman redirects the aircraft so that it can deploy its cargo of Mobiles to the scene of a UFO landing. When Freeman tells him what he has done, Straker is faced with a difficult decision.

Guest stars

John Rutland	**Barnaby Shaw**
Mary Rutland	**Suzanne Neve**
Steven Rutland	**Philip Madoc**
Alien	**Richard Aylen**

ORDEAL

Teleplay **Tony Barwick**
Directed by **Ken Turner**

Following a tour of duty aboard Skydiver, Foster checks in to the SHADO research centre for a routine physical. What begins as a relaxing sauna ends as a nightmare, as Paul finds himself abducted by a couple of Aliens and dragged to their waiting craft. Having been damaged earlier by the Interceptors, the UFO is unable to maintain its flight and is forced to crash-land on the Moon. Following a lucky escape, Foster is rescued and taken back to Moonbase. It is then that the Moonbase personnel are faced with the task of removing him from the Alien spacesuit into which he has been sealed.

Guest stars

Joe Franklin	**David Healy**
Dr. Harris	**Basil Moss**

▼ Acting upon Doctor Jackson's instructions, Gay Ellis prepares to remove the Alien space-suit into which Paul Foster has been sealed. (Ordeal)

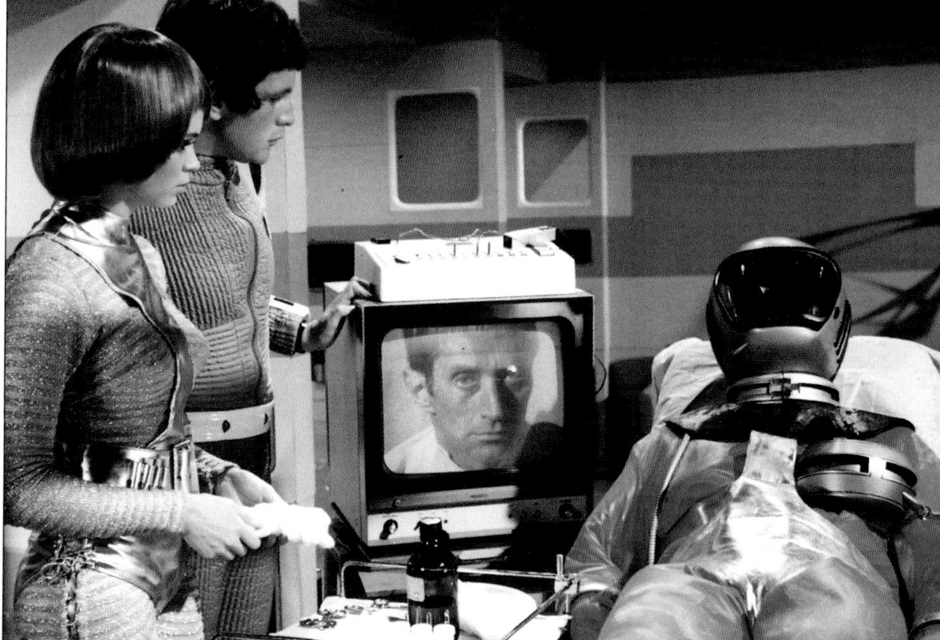

THE RESPONSIBILITY SEAT

Teleplay **Tony Barwick**
Directed by **Alan Perry**

When Jo Fraser, a freelance journalist, makes off with a tape recording which could endanger SHADO's security, Straker goes after her, blaming himself for what has happened. Having been left in charge during Straker's absence, Freeman is faced with a crisis when a mobile Russian drilling rig goes out of control and becomes locked on a collision course with Moonbase. Meanwhile, finding himself attracted to Miss Fraser, Straker takes her back to his house and opens up to her about his failed marriage and feelings of isolation. Unfortunately, as he is to discover, the girl is not all that she claims to be.

Guest stars

Jo Fraser	**Jane Merrow**
Russian astronauts	**Janos Kuracz**
	Paul Tamarin
Russian base commander	**Patrick Jordan**

THE SQUARE TRIANGLE

Teleplay **Alan Pattillo**
Directed by **David Lane**

When Straker allows a UFO to penetrate SHADO's defences in the hope of capturing its occupant, he has no idea of the bizarre situation which will arise. In a remote country house, Liz Newton and her lover, Cass Fowler, plan to shoot Liz's husband when he arrives home from work. Unfortunately for them, it is an Alien who walks through the front door and meets with a sudden and violent end. Foster is soon on the scene and the would-be murderers are taken back to SHADO headquarters and given an amnesia drug. Only then does the truth become clear and Straker realizes that, if he lets them go, he will be condemning Liz's husband to certain death.

Guest stars

Liz Newton	**Adrienne Corri**
Jack Newton	**Allah Cuthbertson**
Cass Fowler	**Patrick Mower**
Alien	**Anthony Chinn**

▲ In a converted conference room, deep within SHADO HQ, Paul Foster faces Jackson's relentless questioning as he stands trial for espionage. (Court Martial)

◀ Watched by her scheming lover, played by Patrick Mower, Liz Newton (Adrienne Corri) ensures that her husband suspects nothing of the murderous trap they intend to spring when he arrives home. (The Square Triangle)

COURT MARTIAL

Teleplay **Tony Barwick**
Directed by **David Lane**

When a security leak endangers Skydiver, the finger of suspicion points at Paul Foster. Another breach of security, this time concerning a Moon flight, and SHADO's newest recruit finds himself facing a charge of espionage. Mounting evidence and Jackson's relentless prosecution leads to a unanimous verdict of guilty – much to Straker's alarm. Believing Foster to be innocent, he and Freeman follow up a slender lead and uncover the proof they need to get the condemned man well and truly off the hook. Unfortunately, during their absence, Foster has escaped from SHADO headquarters and Henderson's orders are that he is to be shot on sight!

Guest stars

Webb	**Jack Hedley**
Carl Mason	**Neil McCallum**
Jane Grant	**Georgina Cookson**
Singleton	**Tutte Lemkow**

▲ Aboard SHADO's Lunar Module, a team of astronauts prepare to fit the special high-powered camera to the modified B142. (Court Martial)

CLOSE UP

Teleplay **Tony Barwick**
Directed by **Alan Perry**

Straker asks the International Astrophysical Commission for one billion dollars to finance the most ambitious project yet undertaken by SHADO. Straker's plan is to equip a B142 space probe with a revolutionary new camera which will allow it to obtain highly detailed photographs of the Alien planet. Despite Henderson's objections, the scheme is approved and before long the specially adapted probe is following a fleeing UFO back to its origin. Four months later, SHADO scanners lock onto the signal for which they have been waiting and, with baited breath, Straker and Freeman stand by as the first pictures come through.

Guest stars

Kelly	**Neil Hallett**
Dr Young	**James Beckett**
Rocket launch controller	**Frank Mann**

CONFETTI CHECK A-OK

Teleplay **Tony Barwick**
Directed by **David Lane**

A special flash-back episode which tells of the formation of SHADO, Straker's dedication to his work and the disasterous affect this has upon his marriage. It is the early 1970s and, on the eve of his honeymoon, Straker is forced to leave his wife, Mary, and travel to New York to address a delegation of government officials. He does a good job in convincing them of the Alien threat and they agree unanimously to set up a highly advanced defence force. Much to Straker's surprise, he is nominated as the commander. As the months roll by, Mary becomes increasingly depressed and suspicious when her husband refuses to tell her where he is spending so much of his time.

Guest stars

Mary	**Suzanne Neve**
Mary's father	**Michael Nightingale**
Doctor	**Tom Oliver**
Estate agent	**Donald Pelmear**

ESP

Teleplay **Alan Fennell**
Directed by **Ken Turner**

Since childhood John Croxley has had the ability

to read the thoughts of others and sense the future. When a speeding UFO manages to evade the Interceptors, Straker can't understand why it crashes into a secluded house, killing the only occupant – Croxley's wife. An injured Paul Foster tells of a strange man observing him in his hospital bed and, when a detailed film script exposing SHADO lands on Straker's desk, the commander and Alec Freeman find themselves caught up in a chain of events which leads them back to the derelict house and an encounter with an unusually perceptive and dangerous opponent.

Guest stars

John Croxley	**John Stratton**
Stella Croxley	**Deborah Stanford**
Dr. Ward	**Douglass Wilmer**
Dr Shroeder	**Maxwell Shaw**

◀ Crippled by an Alien underwater craft, Skydiver sinks fast. As Lt. Barry attends to an injured crewman (Anthony Chin), Straker must overcome his claustrophobia and take charge of the situation. (Sub-Smash)

▼ In the Moonbase Control sphere, Commander Straker faces an unexpected threat – a murder attempt by Paul Foster! (Kill Straker)

KILL STRAKER!

Teleplay **Donald James**
Directed by **Alan Perry**

When an Earth-bound Lunar Module is threatened by an approaching UFO, Straker orders Foster and his co-pilot Frank Craig, to re-enter the atmosphere at an acute angle. The manoeuvre almost certainly saves their lives but, upon recovery, both men are found to have undergone a radical change of personality. First Craig tries to kill Straker by injecting an air-bubble into his bloodstream, then Foster pulls a gun on him when he confronts him in the Moonbase Control sphere. When it becomes apparent that both men have succumbed to Alien brain washing, Straker realizes that he is facing a kill or cure situation and takes a desperate gamble in order to free Paul's mind from the grip of Alien control.

Guest stars

Frank Craig	**David Sumner**
Nurse	**Louise Pajo**

SUB-SMASH

Teleplay **Alan Fennell**
Directed by **David Lane**

When a freighter sinks in mysterious circumstances, Straker believes it to be the work of the Aliens. Leaving Freeman in charge of

SHADO headquarters, the commander joins a hand-picked Skydiver crew as they go in search of the Alien marauder. No sooner has the search begun than they are attacked by a strange underwater craft. Sky One manages to destroy it when it takes off, but then all contact with the crippled submarine is lost. Unable to surface and with only one escape hatch in working order, things look bleak for the trapped crew as both the air and power supplies begin to fade.

Guest stars

Lieutenant Lewis	**Paul Maxwell**
Lieutenant Chin	**Anthony Chinn**
Pilot	**Burnell Tucker**
SHADO Divers	**John Golightly**
	Alan Haywood

THE SOUND OF SILENCE

Teleplay **David Lane and Bob Bell**
Directed by **David Lane**

A secluded lake deep within the English countryside provides the perfect hiding place for a UFO, and the Alien emerges to snatch Russell Stone, an international showjumper whose stables are situated nearby. When SHADO Intelligence receives a report on the missing man, Foster is sent to the stables to investigate. When Stone's sister discovers the decapitated body of a local tramp in the woods, it is enough to convince Foster that an Alien is in the vicinity. Using the Mobiles to depth-charge the lake, Foster watches as the UFO breaks surface and returns fire with frightening accuracy. After a fierce battle the UFO is destroyed – but what is the secret of the canister found floating amongst the debris?

Guest stars

Russell Stone	**Michael Jayston**
Anne Stone	**Susan Jameson**
Cully	**Nigel Gregory**
Alien	**Gito Santana**

THE CAT WITH TEN LIVES

Teleplay David Tomblin
Directed by David Tomblin

Interceptor pilot Jim Regan returns to Earth, looking forward to some peace and quiet. Driving home along a darkened country lane, he and his wife are suddenly attacked by two Aliens and carried into a nearby UFO. The UFO lifts off with Jean aboard but Jim, inexplicably, is left by the roadside together with a Siamese cat which he had found shortly before the abduction took place. As events unfold, it becomes apparent that Jim is, in some way, under the influence of the cat – a revelation which comes too late to prevent him from locking his Interceptor onto a collision course with Moonbase.

Guest stars

Jim Regan	**Alexis Kanner**
Jean Regan	**Geraldine Moffatt**
Albert Thompson	**Colin Gordon**
Muriel Thompson	**Eleanor Summerfield**
Morgan	**Windsor Davis**
Captain Steve Minto	**Steven Berkoff**

▼ Sarah Bosanquet (Stephanie Beacham) mellows out as smooth-talking Paul Foster turns on the charm. (Destruction)

DESTRUCTION

Teleplay **Dennis Spooner**
Directed by **Ken Turner**

Straker is convinced that the Aliens have found a way of slipping past Moonbase undetected and that the aircraft shot down by a Royal Navy vessel was a UFO. Eventually the truth comes to light: the ship is dumping canisters of nerve gas into the sea and, if exposed to the atmosphere, the gas will kill every living being on the planet.

Before the ship can complete its mission, a UFO evades the Interceptors and homes in. As the vessel comes under attack, only Sky One can save mankind from certain extinction.

Guest stars

Sarah Bosanquet	**Stephanie Beacham**
Admiral Sherringham	**Edwin Richfield**
Ship's Captain	**Philip Madoc**
Second Officer Cooper	**Peter Blythe**

THE MAN WHO CAME BACK

Teleplay **Terence Feely**
Directed by **David Lane**

Eight weeks after going missing during a UFO attack, Craig Collins, a top SHADO astronaut, is found apparently unharmed on a remote island. No one is happier at his return than Ed Straker but Virginia Lake insists that he has changed. Collins is immediately assigned to repair SID, which had been badly damaged in the attack, and when Paul Foster is injured during training, Straker agrees to accompany Collins on the mission. As their spaceship heads for the stricken satellite, Straker is unaware that Collins is not the man he used to be and that he is alone in space with an Alien-controlled killer!

Guest stars

Craig Collins	**Derren Nesbit**
Colonel John Grey	**Gary Raymond**
Sir Esmond	**Roland Culver**
Miss Holland	**Lois Maxwell**

REFLECTIONS IN THE WATER

Teleplay **David Tomblin**
Directed by **David Tomblin**

When the freighter *Kingston* is sunk by what the captain describes as 'flying fish', Skydiver is immediately sent to investigate. Narrowly avoiding an undersea UFO, Skydiver locates a huge Alien dome, constructed on the sea bed. Wanting to see it for himself, Straker can't believe his eyes when he looks through a porthole in the side of the dome and sees Lieutenant Anderson, a SHADO Control Room technician who is supposed to be on leave! As the mystery unfolds, Straker and Foster come face to face with a group of Alien *doppelgängers* and discover an ingenious plan to infiltrate SHADO headquarters.

Guest stars

Lieutenant Anderson	**James Cosmo**
Skydiver captain	**David Warbeck**

THE PSYCHOBOMBS

Teleplay **Tony Barwick**
Directed by **Jeremy Summers**

Linda Simmonds, Clem Mason and Daniel Clark, three perfectly ordinary people – until the night a UFO lands, hypnotizes them and embues them all with strange and fantastic powers. Straker can't believe it when the Fairfield tracking station and then Skydiver 3 are blown to pieces – there is nothing to link the two incidents except that a wholly unremarkable civilian was reported on the scene just prior to each disaster. As the truth dawns, Foster makes contact with the last surviving member of the trio and brings her back to SHADO headquarters. Can Straker discover the source of Linda's unearthly powers before she destroys the headquarters and everyone in it?

Guest stars

Linda Simmonds	**Deborah Grant**
Clem Mason	**Mike Pratt**
Daniel Clark	**David Collings**
Captain Lauritzen	**Tom Adams**

▲ Lake and Straker engage in a deadly game of cat and mouse as they persue a treacherous SHADO operative through the sound stages of the Harlington Straker film studios. (Timelash)

◀ Virginia Lake enjoys a tender reunion with Craig Collins (Derrin Nesbitt) following the astronaught's return to Moonbase. (The Man Who Came Back)

TIMELASH

Teleplay **Terrence Feely**
Directed by **Cyrel Frankel**

Straker and Colonel Lake are driving back to SHADO headquarters when a UFO suddenly appears and attacks their car. Miraculously they survive but, arriving back at the studios, they are shocked to discover that everyone and everything is locked in some kind of stasis. Studio workers and SHADO personnel alike stand around like living statues – it's as if time itself has been frozen! Searching for an answer, Straker and Lake are confronted by Turner, a Control Room technician, who has been given immunity by the Aliens in return for his help. As the hovering UFO prepares to land, Straker must find a way of beating an enemy who is always, quite literally, one jump ahead!

Guest star

Turner	**Patrick Allen**

MINDBENDER

Teleplay **Tony Barwick**
Directed by **Ken Turner**

Investigating the mysterious self-destruction of a UFO, Straker and Foster arrive back at Moonbase in time to witness the inexplicable and violent actions of an astronaut who seems to believe that he is surrounded by Mexican bandits. Foster is forced to shoot him in order to save another operative's life. Back on Earth, a headquarters department head becomes afflicted with similar hallucinations Straker experiences the most bizarre perceptual attack of all. During an argument with Henderson, the commander is left reeling when a voice shouts 'cut' and he finds himself standing not in his office but in a brightly lit film set!

Guest stars

Howard Byrne	**Stuart Damon**
Beaver James	**Charles Tingwell**
Andy Conroy	**Al Mancini**
Film director	**Stephen Chase**

THE LONG SLEEP

Teleplay **David Tomblin**
Directed by **Jeremy Summers**

Catherine Fraser has been in a coma for ten years, ever since she was knocked down by a car after running blindly into the road. The driver of the car had been Ed Straker, so, when Catherine regains consciousnes, he insists on being at her bedside. As her memory returns, she remembers how she and her boyfriend, Tim, had been experimenting with drugs when they had come across two 'space men' burying something in a deserted farmhouse. It had all seemed like some hallucination, but, certain that the device had been a massive bomb, Straker urges her to remember the exact details of what she had seen.

Guest Stars

Catherine Fraser	**Tessa Wyatt**
Tim	**Christian Roberts**

▼ Straker does his best to comfort Catherine Frazer (Tessa Wyatt), after she has recovered from a decade-long coma. (The Long Sleep)

▲ Gabrielle Drake, showing a little more leg than usual! With their purple hair and silver cat-suits, the Moonbase girls could have stepped out of any swinging-sixties discoteque!

Chapter 5

The End of the Beginning

At a time when interest in space travel was at its peak due to NASA's frequent manned Moon landings, it must have been difficult for the cast and production team of *UFO* to comprehend that the series failed to receive the prestigious network slot for which it had seemed ideally suited. At a cost of £96,000 per episode, *UFO* was, in 1970, the most expensive and without a doubt the most spectacular science fiction series ever produced in Great Britain and a firm vote of confidence from the ITV schedulers would have gone a long way to insure the future of such ambitious and well-crafted productions. Unfortunately, for reasons unknown even to this day, *UFO* suffered the fate of so many quality programmes and found itself being broadcast to the nation on a rather haphazard schedule. The result of this poor treatment during its initial run on British television is that, today, *UFO* has acquired a very strong cult status, as opposed to the huge following associated with its contemporaries *Star Trek* and *Doctor Who*. Across the Atlantic, the story was a similar one, if only slightly more remarkable.

During the 1971/72 season, *UFO* led the ratings for over four months on PBS channels in both Los Angeles and New York. PBS (or Public Broadcasting Service) stations, it should be pointed out, exist in huge numbers throughout the United States and broadcast independently to the nation until the big networks (ABC, NBC and CBS) take over at 8 pm. Nothing succeeds like success and, with *UFO* a proven ratings winner, the giant American network CBS contacted ITC's New York office, expressing an interest in buying a further series. The prospect of producing a series at the request of a major American buyer was an exciting one in the extreme, not least of all because of the huge financial rewards, and Gerry Anderson immediately set to work on the planning of what was provisionally to be called *UFO 2*.

▲ Paul Foster seems unconcerned as a last minute adjustment is made to the helmet of his Alien friend!

Aware that those episodes set on the Moon had proved to be the most popular, Gerry decided to dispense with the Earth-based locations and develop the Moonbase concept even further. In the revised format, SHADO was to move its entire operation to a greatly enlarged moonbase (now called Moon City) and would combat the Alien threat with a number of laser equipped space fighters known as Eagles. To incorporate this new development, the events would take place more than a quarter of a century into the future and, as pre-production reached an advanced stage, the title of the new series became *UFO:1999*.

Principle cast members such as Ed Bishop were contacted and told that they had the amber (if not green) light and new story consultant Christopher Penfold was brought in to oversee the commissioning and writing of the 26 scripts which would shortly be required. All systems were go. Then, as zero hour approached, count-down was suddenly and irreversibly suspended. Having led the ratings for 17 consecutive weeks, *UFO*'s popularity began to wane towards the end of its run and, as advertisers began to look elsewhere, CBS changed their minds and decided that they would not after all be purchasing the new and undoubtedly very expensive series. Without the much-needed US backing, another series of *UFO* was deemed to be a very risky proposition and, despite the amount of work that had been put into it, the plug was pulled. Thus today, the series must be judged upon the merits of the 26 episodes produced between May 1969 and October 1970.

▲ This sequence from 'The Responsibility Seat' featuring Jane Merrow and Ed Bishop, resulted in a late night transmission for the episode.

'When I see episodes from the series today,' comments Art Director Bob Bell, 'I am truly surprised by what was achieved. The special effects were certainly ahead of their time and laid the path for all the great effects films that followed.' Without a doubt, the model effects were far in advance of anything else being produced for television in either the UK or America and, in many cases, of a higher standard than those produced for the cinema. Those sequences which take place on Earth, in real environments, are particularly realistic: so much so that it would be difficult to improve upon them, even with today's advanced techniques.

The writing and direction were of a very high standard and, particularly in the case of the later episodes, combined to make a series which, in every respect, challenged the viewer and demanded that it be taken seriously. Of course, this was not without its problems and perhaps contributed to the series failing to achieve a network slot. Where, for example, could you put a series which told a fairly straightforward story of Alien intrusion one week whilst dealing almost exclusively with the domestic problems of its principal character the next? The answer was that it turned up at odd times all over the place; in the more extreme cases, certain episodes were held back for two years before finally being transmitted at an unsuitably late hour.

Of an equally high standard were the actors, particularly the regular cast, who appeared to care enough about what they were doing to turn in performances of a quality which, quite simply, is not often seen in even the best examples of the genre today. Ed Bishop, in particular, seemed to get right inside the skin of Ed Straker and today, even without his blond wig and futuristic suits, the actor is still recognized in the street for the character he portrayed almost a quarter of a century ago!

Perhaps the single most interesting aspect of the series, however, is the picture it paints of a future world – the world of 1980 as imagined from a 1960's standpoint. America's influence on that world is shown to have reached epic proportions and, even in Great Britain, the dollar has become the accepted form of currency and everyone drives what appear to be American cars on the right hand side of the road. Racial prejudice is also something of the past, having burned itself out, according to the episode 'Survival', in the mid-1970s. If this seems a little optimistic, then it is made clear that not all the world's differences have been peacefully resolved as, according to a newspaper headline, Russia and China appear to be engaged in hostilities of one sort or another.

Today, the programme is regarded as one of Gerry Anderson's finest achievements and boasts a hardcore of dedicated fans, many of whom belong to Fanderson, the official Gerry Anderson appreciation society. The society has already published a heavily illustrated design file (featuring fine examples of *UFO*'s pre-production artwork), produced a highly informative video documentary and organized several *UFO* conventions, which have attracted both fans and various members of the cast and production team.

In 1994 its many fans celebrate the programme's twenty-fifth anniversary, it should be remembered that not only did *UFO* set new standards when it came to model-filming and special effects, but that it also paved the way for another series which, as events turned out, would prove to be even more spectacular and successful than its predecessor.

▲ As the interceptors prepare to blast off, a new series waits patiently on the launch pad...

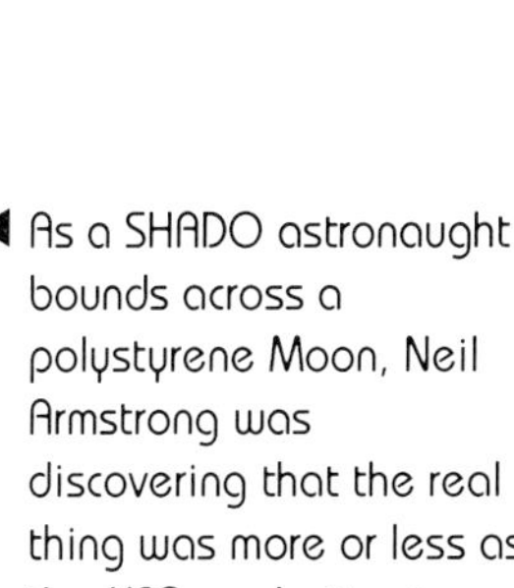

◀ As a SHADO astronaught bounds across a polystyrene Moon, Neil Armstrong was discovering that the real thing was more or less as the *UFO* production team had imagined it.

SPACE: 1999

▲ Barbara Bain and Martin Landau. After lengthy negotiations, the well-known husband and wife team were signed up to play Doctor Helena Russell and Commander John Koenig.

Chapter 6

The Void Ahead

Since the dawn of time, man has gazed up into the night sky and regarded the Moon, our planet's solitary natural satellite, with a mixture of wonderment and awe. Its movements control the tides and, according to some, have an equally strong affect on the human psyche. As the 1960s drew to a close, man finally set foot on his nearest neighbour and an exciting new age of space exploration had begun. As scientists planned to colonize the barren rock and exploit its natural resources, a much smaller team drew up their own plans, ensuring that the moon, in the not too distant future, would become the scene of mankind's greatest ever adventure.

Whilst he had been working on the format for what would have been the second series of *UFO*, Gerry Anderson had been instructed by Abe Mandel (head of ITC in New York) that if the project was to have their full backing then it must be bigger, better and in every way more spectacular than the series from which it was to evolve. Despite the enormity of this request, Gerry rose to the challenge and came up with a scenario which would see the Aliens blasting the Moon out of Earth's orbit and sending it, complete with Commander Straker and SHADO's massive base, on an incredible and unstoppable journey into the depths of outer space.

It was a remarkable concept, and provided an ideal opportunity for the kind of spectacular adventures the Americans seemed to want. When it became apparent that *UFO:1999* (as it was by then to be called) would not be going into production, Gerry convinced Lew Grade that, with some drastic rewriting, the work they had already done would not have to go to waste and that a completely new series could be developed.

UFO:1999 became *Space Journey: 1999* and during the summer of 1973 Gerry and Sylvia Anderson wrote a new pilot script entitled 'Zero G'. With much of the UFO element removed, the script centred around Commander Steve Maddox and the personnel of the now largely scientific Moon City. Following an attack by a hostile alien race, the Moon's gravity is reduced to zero, causing it to drift out of Earth's orbit and begin its incredible voyage.

With high hopes of achieving an American network sale, ITC New York insisted that American writer George Bellak was brought in to act as script editor on the series, thus ensuring that the stories developed in a way that would be acceptable to an American audience. Although Bellak had an extremely good working relationship with Story Consultant Christopher Penfold, his views differed considerably to those of Gerry Anderson and, having re-written the pilot episode as 'The Void Ahead', Bellak left the production. As the incoming scripts began to pile up, Penfold replaced Bellak with another American, Edward di Lorenzo and Irish poet Johnny Byrne. Between them, Byrne and di Lorenzo would see to it that all the commissioned scripts fitted their requirements, as well as making significant story contributions themselves.

As the writing effort progressed, so many changes were made to the format and to the characters contained therein. Moon City had now become Moonbase Alpha and control of the complex was now firmly in the hands of Commander John Koenig. Doctor Helena Russell and Professor Victor Bergman were written in as principal supporting characters, whilst the remainder of the command team comprised chief pilot Alan Carter, Main Mission controller Paul Morrow, data analyst Sandra Benes and, assisting Helena in the medical centre, Doctor Bob Mathias.

As the cast of characters began to develop, so Gerry and Sylvia Anderson were hard at work finding the right actors to bring the personnel of Moonbase Alpha to life. Clearly the most important positions to fill would be those of Commander John Koenig and Doctor Helena Russell. At the request of ITC, the Andersons broke with tradition and, for the first time in their career, went after a couple of big-name American stars, a move which it was hoped would provide the key to the US network.

During their visit to the United States, the Andersons met the popular husband and wife team of Martin Landau and Barbara

▶ The well respected Barry Morse joined the series as Professor Victor Bergman and quickly put his colleagues at ease with his gentle and reassuring presence.

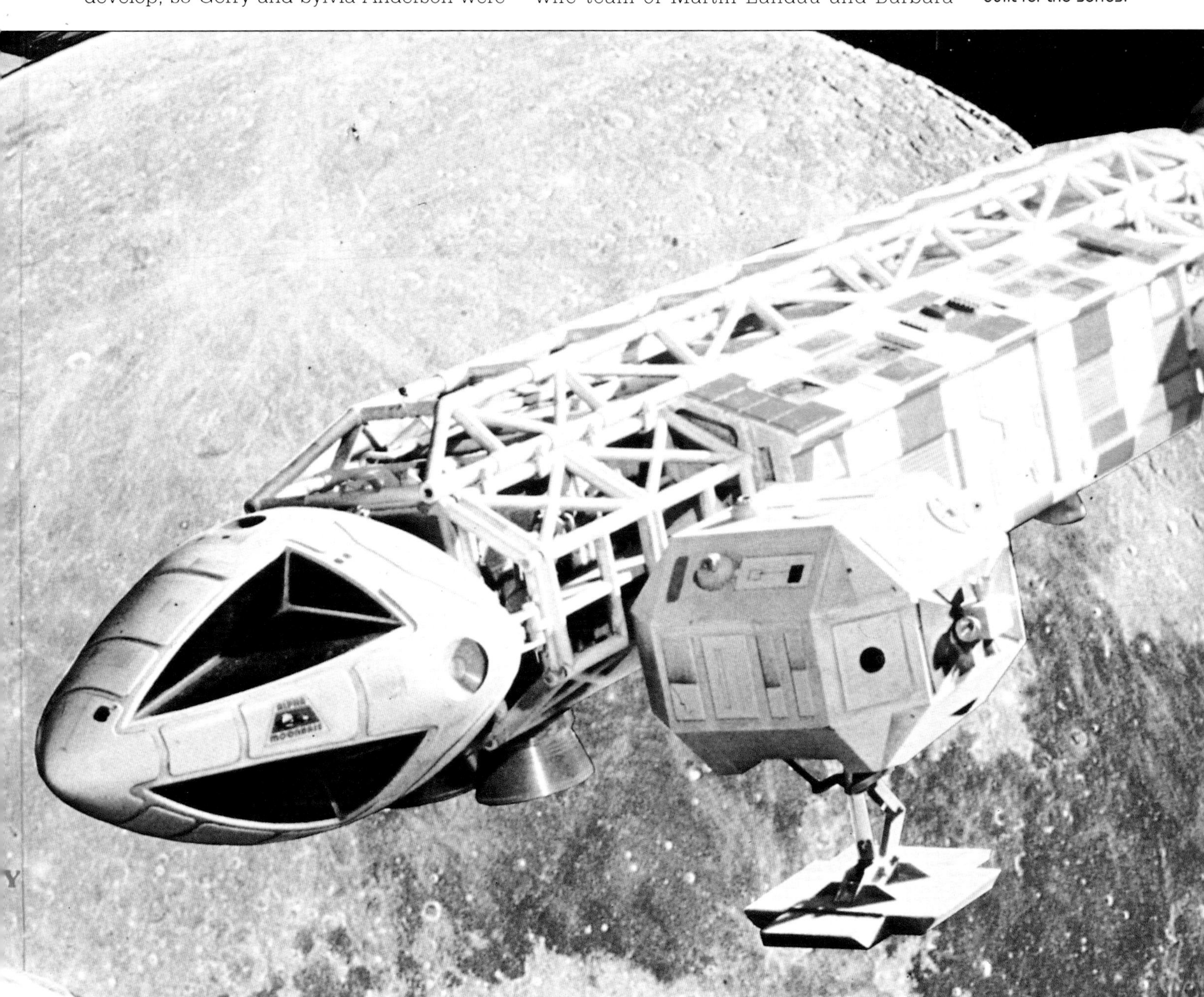

▼ Suspended before a large fibreglass Moon is Brian Johnson's finely detailed Rescue Eagle – one of many variously scaled models built for the series.

Bain, both of whom were actors of some repute, having appeared in a great number of successful films, stage plays and television series, including *Mission: Impossible*, in which they had starred together during the late 1960s. The Landaus were immediately fascinated and impressed by the intriguing scenario and, much to everyone's pleasure, they were happy to commit themselves whole-heartedly to the exciting new venture.

One of the things that had convinced the Landaus to sign up for the show was the assurance that it would feature the most spectacular visual effects ever seen on television. It was a big promise to make, but one that the Andersons were confident they could follow up. Convincing model work had always been a trademark of the Andersons' work and, with well over a decade of experience behind him, Gerry was determined that *Space:1999* (as the show was now called) would put everything else well and truly in the shade. Seeing to it that the series lived up to Gerry's expectations, Production Designer Keith Wilson and Special Effects supervisor Brian Johnson worked tirelessly at entirely different locations deep within the countryside of rural Buckinghamshire.

At Pinewood Studios, where the

A close-up of the Commlocks.

live-action element of the series was to be filmed, Keith Wilson had designed and constructed a revolutionary modular set which would soon become the futuristic interior of Moonbase Alpha. Built entirely from durable sheets of plastic, the space-age set could be fitted together in a variety of different configurations, thus allowing the same panels to be used for the basis of Main Mission, the medical centre, sections of corridor or any number of other rooms or areas as they were required. Wilson was also responsible for designing the highly original commlocks and hand-held laser weapons which would be just as vital to the personnel of Moonbase Alpha as the base itself or their fleet of spaceworthy hardware.

As the main unit prepared to go into production at Pinewood, the special effects unit, based at a much smaller studio in nearby Bray, put the finishing touches to the impressive models which would be so integral to the success of the forthcoming series. With Derek Meddings now working in feature films, the Special Effects supervisor for *SPACE:1999* was Brian Johnson, a talented young craftsman who had previously worked for Gerry on *Thunderbirds* before moving on to design and build all the spaceships for Stanley Kubrick's epic production of *2001: A Space Odyssey*. Bringing with him the basic design of what would become Moonbase Alpha, Johnson's crowning achievement whilst working on the series was to be the design of the Eagles; the multipurpose spacecraft which would provide the personnel of Moonbase Alpha with a means of interplanetary transport as well as a formidable deterrent against alien attack.

On Monday 11 November 1973, on Stage M at Pinewood Studios, filming began on what was undoubtedly the most ambitious science-fiction series ever to go before the

▲ Brian Johnson's Moonbase Alpha. An integral part of *Space:1999*.

▲ **Above left:** Martin Landau, seated at Commander Koenig's desk. To the right is Commissioner Simmonds (Roy Dotrice) and the impressive Main Mission set can be seen in the background.

cameras in Great Britain. With a budget well in excess of three million pounds, it was also the most expensive. Credited as a Group Three Production (Group Three being the name of the production company headed by Gerry and Sylvia Anderson and longtime associate Reg Hill), the series was co-financed by ITC and the Italian television network RAI, a move which explains the number of Italian guest stars who appear in prominent roles in several episodes of the first series.

As for the remainder of the series' regular cast: well-known British actor Barry Morse joined Martin Landau and Barbara Bain as the thoughtful Professor Victor Bergman, whilst Nick Tate, Prentis Hancock, Zienia Merton and Anton Philips were cast as Alan Carter, Paul Morrow, Sandra Benes and Doctor Bob Mathias respectively. They would be joined in the second episode, 'Matter of Life and Death', by Clifton Jones as computer operator David Kano.

As the cameras rolled, so the Moon left Earth's orbit – hurled on its way by a massive explosion of man's own making. The journey had begun, but no one, not even Gerry Anderson, could know exactly what lay ahead...

▶ In their small workshop in Bray, Nick Adler and Brian Johnson supervise the construction of the many Eagles and miniature installations which the series will require.

▲ On the dark side of the Moon, an Eagle hovers above one of the nuclear waste dumps.

Chapter 7

Destination Moonbase Alpha

By the end of the twentieth century, interplanetary space travel has become a reality and man is taking his first tentative steps towards the stars. Vital to the existing and future space programme is Moonbase Alpha, a self-contained lunar complex from where an élite scientific community probes the unknown, paving the way for the deep-space pioneers who it is hoped will follow in their wake.

Situated within the crater Copernicus, close to the Ocean of Storms, Moonbase Alpha is a circular collection of laboratories, workshops and living areas with an overall diameter of two and a half miles. At the centre of the complex stands Alpha's command post, the ten storey Main Mission tower, whilst outlying buildings and launch pads are connected to the main assembly by a network of spoke-like travel tubes. With nuclear generating facilities, an oxygen/water recycling plant and a well established hydroponics farm, Moonbase Alpha was designed to be completely self-supporting; a precaution which was to ensure the survival of its personnel following its dramatic and unforeseen departure from Earth's orbit on 13 September, 1999.

Authorized by the World Space Commission, work began on the construction of Moonbase Alpha in February 1983, but was halted during the devastating thermonuclear war of 1987. When peace was finally declared, the world that emerged from the holocaust was a very different place. There would be no more wars – the planet couldn't survive another global conflict. Instead the people of Earth united to create a more enlightened, scientific society. Those nuclear weapons that remained were dismantled, their radioactive warheads sealed in special containers, and then, along with every other kind of nuclear waste, they were buried in deep wells on the inhospitable dark side of the Moon. As work on Moonbase Alpha recommenced, so it became the symbol of the new united Earth – a place where scientists from every nation could work together for the ultimate good of mankind.

▲ A lunar excursion for a team of Moonbase astronauts. Alpha's outlying buildings can be seen in the background.

By the mid-1990s, Moonbase Alpha was fully staffed and operational, with every one of its 311 personnel being attached to a designated section or department where their individual skills could be put to good use. As a security measure, everyone on Alpha is provided with a colour-coded uniform; the colour of the left sleeve corresponding with the section in which he or she is authorized to work.

By far the largest proportion of Alpha's personnel belong to the Technical section,

▲ Doctor Helena Russell, a compassionate friend and expert in all areas of space medicine.

who not only have their own section block, but are also responsible for maintaining the base's life-support systems and ensuring that the fleet of Eagle spaceships is kept in good working order. Working alongside the Technical staff in their laboratories and computer rooms are the men and women of the Service section. Often overlooked by their loftier colleagues, it is the responsibility of the Service personnel to attend to the more mundane aspects of base maintenance, such as data correlation and running the Alpha laundry service. On the periphery of the base, stand the five circular launch pads, from which Alpha's fleet of fifty Eagle transporters operate. Housed in massive underground hangers, the Eagles not only provide the base with an efficient and reusable form of transport, but, when equipped with lasers, are transformed into a formidable means of defence. Weighing 328 tons and driven by nuclear-fusion engines, the Eagle is essentially a skeletal lifting-body, into which a variety of different utility modules can be attached. The standard passenger module is designed to hold up to ten people, whilst modules fitted with computer or medical equipment will enable the Eagle to be used as a reconnaissance or rescue vehicle. Crewed by pilots from the Reconnaissance section, the Eagles have proved themselves time and time again and, when the time comes to evacuate Moonbase Alpha, it is the Eagle transporters which will carry the personnel safely to their new home.

Considerably smaller but equally as important are the hand-held commlocks which are issued to everyone as soon as they arrive on Moonbase Alpha. Personalized and

◀ The Moonbase sidearm. Known to everyone as a 'stun gun', this versatile weapon can be put to a number of different uses.

◀ Commander John Koenig. A strong but sensitive leader, Koenig quickly developed a soft spot for Doctor Russell.

worn clipped to the belt, each commlock combines a number of functions, most notably those of an audio/visual communicator and electronic key, and allows its owner to enter designated areas of the base, according to his or her rank, position or security clearance. Powered by a rechargeable energy cell, the commlock can be plugged into a desk-top terminal for recharging and can also be used as a digital chronometer, personal computer or emergency alarm transmitter.

Issued on a strictly limited basis are the powerful laser/stun-gun weapons, which are carried permanently by no one except Alpha's purple-sleeved contingent of security personnel. Fitted with four snub-nosed barrels, the weapon is capable of firing three laser beams of varying destructive power, and, if set to stun, a passive light ray from the first barrel can be used to direct a 14,000 volt electrical discharge at any living target. Although use of the weapons is restricted on Moonbase Alpha, they are carried as standard equipment on all Eagles and have proven to be life-savers in hostile situations.

In the sterile atmosphere of the base, colds and other viral infections are almost unknown; psychological and physical disorders are, however, a very real danger when living and working in what is, after all, an unnatural and unchanging environment. For this reason, chief medical officer Helena Russell carries out regular check-ups on every man and woman on the base and encourages everyone to take full advantage of the extensive recreational facilities that the base provides, which include a bowling alley, cinema, gymnasium, solarium and a well-stocked library. As an added precaution, everyone wears a 'wrist-watch' medical monitor, which raises the alarm if the wearer suffers injury or exhibits any kind of abnormal changes in pulse rate, respiration or brain activity.

Without doubt, Moonbase Alpha is an elaborate and impressive complex; but what of the men and women who make up its small but essential command team? They may be small in number, but their skills are great and each one of them is vital to the smooth running of the base.

Colleagues In Command

COMMANDER JOHN KOENIG

Born in Brooklyn in 1959, John Robert Koenig developed a fascination for space-travel from watching the Apollo space missions of the late 1960s and like so many others, hoped that one day he would be able to journey into space himself. His dream came true in the early 1980s when, as an ambitious NASA cadet, he planned and flew a number of important deep space missions. Assigned to Moonbase Alpha's Reconnaissance section in 1996, Koenig was responsible for setting up the ill-fated Ultra Probe mission which ended in disaster for the crew and a temporary grounding for himself. Returning to Alpha on 9 September 1999 Koenig was unable to prevent the massive nuclear cataclysm which, four days later, blasted the Moon out of Earth's orbit into deep space.

▲ Alan Carter (Nick Tate), Alpha's chief pilot was never happier than when he was at the controls of an Eagle.

A sensitive and courageous leader, Koenig takes a deep and genuine interest in the lives of every man and woman under his command and, as the drifting Moon encounters numerous unforeseen dangers, so he is prepared to take great personal risks in order to guarantee their safety.

DOCTOR HELENA RUSSELL

An expert in the field of space medicine, Doctor Helena Susan Russell is an invaluable member of Alpha's staff, responsible for the physical and psychological welfare of everyone on the base.

The daughter of a physician, Helena was born in Chicago, Illinois in August 1960. Following in her father's footsteps, she entered the medical profession at an early age and soon joined the Medical Authority of the World Space Commission. An extremely sensitive woman, Helena is very sympathetic to the individual needs of her patients and, short of endangering her own life, she will go to almost any length to ensure their complete wellbeing.

PROFESSOR VICTOR BERGMAN

Born in London in 1940, Victor Bergman graduated from Cambridge University to become one of the most accomplished scientists of his generation, making many great advances, particularly in the fields of physics and electronic engineering. Having helped considerably in the design of Moonbase Alpha, Bergman attached himself to the base in the capacity of non-assigned scientific advisor – his uncoloured uniform denoting his civilian status.

Following the Moon's departure from Earth, Victor, more than anyone else, seem enthralled by the wonders of deep space and the incredible environments through which they pass. Tragically, for the professor the voyage is a short one as, less than a year after breakaway, a malfunction in his artificial heart brings his brilliant life to a premature end.

CAPTAIN ALAN CARTER

Chief pilot and head of the Reconnaissance section, easy-going Australian Alan Carter has clocked-up more space-miles than anyone else on Alpha and is never more at home than when he is safely at the controls of one of his beloved Eagle craft.

Born in Sydney in December 1969, Alan developed a love for flying at an early age

▲ Just like Commander Koenig, Main Mission controller Paul Morrow (Prentis Hancock) often hid his warm nature beneath a somewhat abrasive exterior.

and, leaving his parents' cattle ranch, served as a pilot in the Australian navy before joining the joint US/Australian space programme in 1994. After a number of successful deep-space missions, Alan was assigned to Moonbase Alpha and the exploratory mission planned to investigate the newly discovered planet Meta.

A popular and essential member of the personnel, Carter's value to the base is beyond doubt, for if the people of Alpha are ever likely to find a new home, then it is almost certainly Alan who will fly them there!

PAUL MORROW

Born in London in 1970, Paul Morrow embarked upon his chosen career as a cadet in the European Space Exploration Programme, where his natural leadership qualities were soon spotted and he was assigned to the newly completed Moonbase Alpha in 1994 as controller of the installation's nerve centre, Main Mission.

Wearing the flame-coloured sleeve associated with the post, Morrow cuts an authoritative figure and makes the ideal deputy for Koenig during the Commander's absence from the base. Appearing somewhat stern and abrupt in manner, Morrow's hard exterior belies a softer centre. Although he seldom let it show whilst on duty, it was no secret that for quite some time he was romantically linked with data analyst Sandra Benes and one day the couple had hoped to start a family. Unfortunately the opportunity was never to arise as, like Victor Bergman, Paul was to die in tragic circumstances barely twelve months after the Moon had begun its galactic voyage.

SANDRA BENES

One of the quieter members of the command team, data analyst Sandra Benes wears the yellow sleeve of the Service section although, as section-head, her duties confine her to the nerve centre of the complex where she is responsible for controlling Alpha's powerful and sophisticated communications system.

Following the death of Paul Morrow in an Eagle crash, Sandra turned to Buddhism in the hope of finding spiritual peace and enlightenment and, in an effort to forget the past, she cast out all personal possessions and changed her name to Sahn – a decision which was both supported and respected by every one of her friends and closest colleagues.

▼ The quiet Sandra Benes (Zienia Merton) was in charge of Main Mission's communication system. Off-duty, she shared a close relationship with her colleague Paul Morrow.

◀ On the planet Zenno, Raan (Peter Cushing), Vana (Joanna Dunham) and Sandra appear to Commander Koenig from a mysterious ethereal mist. (Missing Link)

Chapter 8

The Journey Begins

Moonbase Alpha's journey through space was to last for a total of 48 episodes, making up two seasons of 24 episodes apiece. As with *UFO*, each episode had an approximate running time of between 45 and 50 minutes.

Although changes were made between seasons, every episode of the first season began with a short 'teaser' or hook, which, having built up to a dramatic climax, would give way to what is generally regarded as the most exciting and spectacular title sequence ever devised for a British television show.

Following the introduction of series' stars, Martin Landau and Barbara Bain, courtesy of moodily lit close-ups, the programme's title seems to materialize above a panoramic shot of Moonbase Alpha. Then the fun begins! Like a bizarre hovering insect, an Eagle transporter hangs suspended against the star-studded sky before falling, like a stone , and exploding spectacularly against the barren lunar surface. Backed by a driving up-tempo theme, shots from the following episode are edited, on the beat, to form a dazzling preview of the excitement to come. A slower, orchestral middle section accompanies the introduction of actor Barry Morse and producer/executive producer credits, before the tempo is taken up again for a final sequence of shots showing the awesome explosion which pushes the Moon out of Earth's orbit. The programme's closing credits are displayed against a number of picturesque space panoramas and are accompanied by a much shorter, predominantly orchestral arrangement of the main theme.

◀ In Main Mission, all eyes are on the big screen as signals come through from the planet Meta. (Breakaway)

This chapter covers the 24 episodes that make up the first season and presents them, for the first time, in their actual order of production, which differs considerably from the order in which they were eventually broadcast. The first episode, 'Breakaway' was transmitted by ATV on 4 September, 1975, whilst 'The Last Enemy' brought the first series to an end on 19 February, 1976 – almost a month after filming had begun on 'The Metamorph', the first episode of the heavily revamped second season.

BREAKAWAY

Screenplay by **George Bellak**
Directed by **Lee H. Katzin**

A mysterious illness is wiping out the crew of a deep space probe destined for the newly

▲ Koenig and Victor interrogate Lee Russell (Richard Johnson) in the hope of discovering if he really is the man he claims to be. (Matter of Life and Death)

discovered planet Meta. With the mission in jeopardy, John Koenig arrives on Moonbase Alpha to assume command – his orders are to resolve the problem and see that the Meta probe is launched. Discovering that magnetic emissions from the nearby nuclear waste dumps are the most likely cause, Koenig requests that shipment of waste should be temporarily suspended. His request is denied and it isn't long before the smaller of the two sites energizes and explodes. As a massive heat increase is detected in the much larger second site, Koenig orders immediate dispersal of the buried waste containers. But it is too late. An explosion of unbelievable force annihilates the waste site and blasts the moon out of Earth's orbit.

Guest Stars

Commissioner Simmonds	**Roy Dotrice**
Commander Gorski	**Philip Madoc**
Ben Ouma	**Lon Satton**
Tanya Alexander	**Suzanne Roquette**

MATTER OF LIFE AND DEATH

Screenplay **Art Wallace and Johnny Byrne**
Directed by **Charles Crichton**

A mystery of great complexity unfolds when the unconscious body of Lee Russell, Helena's long-lost husband, is discovered aboard an Eagle returning from an apparently Earth-like planet. Upon recovery, Lee cannot explain how he came to be there and Koenig's suspicions are aroused when a thermographic examination reveals the man to be something other than human. When

Koenig ignores Lee's warnings to stay away from the planet, the man dies and, much to his alarm, Victor discovers that the body is transforming into anti-matter. Venturing down to the planet with a landing party, Helena can only watch helplessly as her colleagues die in a series of inexplicable accidents and then the Moon itself explodes. As she huddles amidst the desolation, distraught and alone, her 'husband' suddenly appears and offers the Alphans a second chance.

Guest Stars

Lee Russell	**Richard Johnson**
Parks	**Stuart Damon**

BLACK SUN

Screenplay by **David Weir**
Directed by **Lee H. Katzin**

The entire Moon is threatened when it becomes trapped by the gravitational pull of a black sun - a mysterious hole within the very fabric of space from which nothing, not even light, can escape. Unaware of what may lie within or beyond this amazing phenomenon, Koenig orders a small group of Alphans to escape in an Eagle whilst Victor develops a powerful force-field which he hopes will save the base from the incredible crushing forces which they know to expect. As the Moon approaches the hole, Koenig and Bergman sit alone in a deserted Main Mission and prepare for the inevitable. When it comes, the journey through the galactic whirlpool proves to be an amazing and extremely enlightening experience.

Guest Stars

Mike Ryan	**Paul Jones**
Smitty	**John Laurimore**

RING AROUND THE MOON

Screenplay **Edward di Lorenzo**
Directed by **Ray Austin**

The Moon is gripped by a powerful force field and a disembodied voice announces that the personnel of Moonbase Alpha are now prisoners of the planet Triton. Following an unsuccessful attempt by Alan Carter to reach the glowing sphere which suddenly appears close to the Moon, Helena is transformed into a living link between Alpha's main computer and what turns out to be a Tritonian probe. As she transmits vital information to the probe at incredible speed, Koenig and Bergman realize that her brain will be burned out within a matter of hours unless the link can be severed. With the aid of a special antigravity screen, Koenig and Carter set out in an Eagle and attempt to penetrate the Tritonian force field – the question is, will they make it in time to save Helena?

Guest Star

Ted Clifford	**Max Faulkner**

◀ Koenig undergoes a dramatic transformation as Moonbase Alpha reaches the heart of the hole in space. (Black Sun)

EARTHBOUND

Screenplay **Anthony Terpiloff**
Directed by **Charles Crichton**

When a spacecraft crash-lands on the Moon, the cryogenically suspended occupants introduce themselves as Kaldorians and announce that they are on their way to Earth, hoping to make it their new home.

Commissioner Simmonds (who up until now has been keeping a low profile) tries to persuade Koenig to hijack the ship so that at least six of them may return home. Koenig refuses and instead makes a deal with the Kaldorian leader, Captain Zantor, to allow one computer-selected Alphan to accompany them on the journey back to Earth. Simmonds, however, will stop at nothing to ensure that he is the one who returns home and, gaining access to the reactor room, threatens to destroy Alpha unless he is chosen.

Guest Stars

Captain Zantor	**Christopher Lee**
Commissioner Simmonds	**Roy Dotrice**

ANOTHER TIME, ANOTHER PLACE

Screenplay **Johnny Byrne**
Directed by **David Tomblin**

The Moon hits a rift in the fabric of space, which results in it travelling millions of kilometres in a matter of seconds. When the Moon goes into orbit around a strangely familiar planet, the Alphans can't believe it when the computer confirms that the planet is Earth. Their euphoria is short-lived, however, when they discover another identical Moon – complete with a deserted Moonbase Alpha – and realize that they have jumped forward along their own time-line and have somehow got caught up with the future versions of themselves. With the twin Moons locked on a collision course, Koenig has no choice but to order the immediate evacuation of Alpha – unsure of the consequences should the duplicate personnel meet.

Guest Star

Regina Kesslann	**Judy Geeson**

MISSING LINK

Screenplay **Edward di Lorenzo**
Directed by **Ray Austin**

When an Eagle crash-lands on the Moon, the crew, consisting of Koenig, Bergman, Alan Carter and Sandra Benes are injured – Koenig quite badly. As Helena maintains a vigil by Koenig's bedside, puzzled and concerned by his comatose condition, she is unaware that he is nothing more than a projection – his real self having been transported five million light years across

▲ Captain Zantor (Christopher Lee) and his fellow travellers reveal their benevolent intentions to the people of Moonbase Alpha. (Earthbound)

space to the beautiful planet of Zenno. On Zenno, Koenig encounters Raan, an incredibly old anthropologist who believes that the Commander represents the missing link in the evolutionary chain of his own people. By studying Koenig he hopes to discover something about his planet's long forgotten past.

Guest Stars

Raan	**Peter Cushing**
Vana	**Joanna Dunham**

GUARDIAN OF PIRI

Screenplays **Christopher Penfold**
Directed by **Charles Crichton**

At last the Alphans appear to have found their new home. The tranquil planet of Piri offers them everything they need for a leisurely and trouble-free existence. As his entire crew seems to slip into a hypnotic state of euphoria, Koenig remains sceptical, certain that something is wrong. On the planet's surface, the Commander meets an incredibly beautiful girl who introduces herself as the Servant of the Guardian and explains that the people of Alpha have been drawn here to relieve their suffering. Koenig is unconvinced, realizing that the blissful life they have been promised is nothing more than a living death. As his own people turn against him, Koenig must take drastic action in order to expose the planet for what it really is.

Guest Stars

Servant of the Guardian	**Catherine Schell**
Eagle Pilot	**Gareth Hunt**

FORCE OF LIFE

Screenplay **Johnny Byrne**
Directed by **David Tomblin**

A ball of intense blue light flashes towards Moonbase Alpha and, as time itself is suspended, the light-being enters the body of reactor technician Anton Zoref. Unable to keep warm, Zoref develops an insatiable desire for heat and, leaving a trail of bodies and drained equipment in his wake, he stalks Alpha, drawing the energy he needs from any source available. As the situation becomes desperate, Koenig orders a complete power-cut in all sections of the base, in the hope of depriving Zoref of the energy he needs. The technician proves difficult to stop and, as Alpha begins to freeze, he manages to force his way into a nuclear reactor.

Guest Stars

Anton Zoref	**Ian McShane**
Eva Zoref	**Gay Hamilton**

On the paradise world of Piri, Koenig has a hard job convincing his friends that things aren't quite as rosy as they seem. (Guardian of Piri)

ALPHA CHILD

Screenplay **Christopher Penfold**
Directed by **Ray Austin**

A momentous occasion for Moonbase Alpha – the arrival of the first child to be born on the Moon – quickly turns into a nightmare when the baby grows into a 5 year-old boy within a matter of minutes. Helena is unable to explain his incredible growth rate and, when the boy draws a highly detailed picture of an advanced spaceship, Koenig becomes increasingly suspicious. Suddenly, four spaceships,

Pulling a face guaranteed to win Moonbase Alpha's gurning competition, Anton Zoref (Ian McShane) realizes that his body has been invaded by a cold-hearted intruder. (Force of Life)

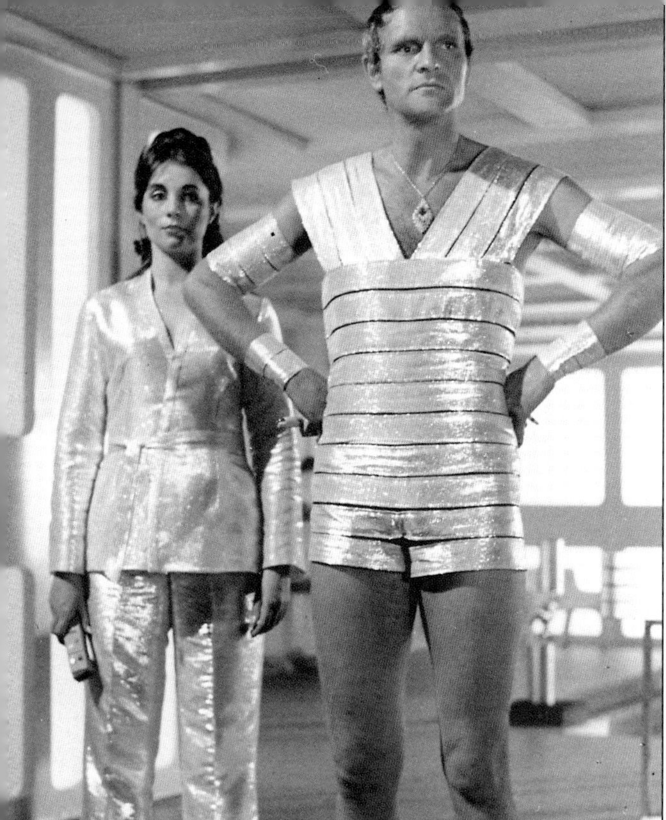

identical to the one in Jackie's drawing, appear and take up positions above the base. As Koenig prepares to lead an attack, Jackie transforms into a fully grown man and reveals his terrifying plans for the people of Alpha.

Guest Stars

Jarak	**Julian Glover**
Cynthia Crawford	**Cyd Hayman**
Jackie Crawford	**Wayne Brooks**

THE LAST SUNSET

Screenplay **Christopher Penfold**
Directed by **Charles Crichton**

As the Moon approaches the planet Ariel the unbelievable happens: hundreds of small probes from the planet land close to Alpha and exude fresh air. As the Moon gains an atmosphere, the crew of Moonbase Alpha rush out on to the surface, basking in the warm sun and gazing up into a clear blue sky! The sudden and miraculous transformation is not without its dangers, however, and on a reconnaissance mission, an Eagle is caught in a violent thunder storm and forced to crash land. With their radio smashed and provisions contaminated, Helena, Paul, Sandra and Alan realize that, unless they are found soon, even their newly acquired atmosphere will not save them from a certain death.

VOYAGER'S RETURN

Screenplay **Johnny Byrne**
Directed by **Bob Kellett**

Voyager One, a deep-space probe launched from Earth in 1985, is detected on a collision course with the Moon. When a reconnaissance Eagle ventures too close to the probe, it is destroyed by the deadly neutron wake produced by the vehicle's revolutionary propulsion system. Doctor Ernst Queller, designer of the probe's drive unit, reveals himself and offers to deactivate the system. He does so, allowing the probe to be safely brought down to Alpha. As Professor Bergman prepares to access Voyager's data bank, three space-ships from the planet Sidon appear and streak towards Alpha – their mission, the annihilation of humanity in revenge for the destruction wrought upon them by the space probe.

Guest Stars

Dr Ernst Linden/Queller	**Jeremy Kemp**
Jim Haines	**Barry Stokes**
Steve Abrams	**Lawrence Trimble**
Aarchon	**Alex Scott**

◀ Jarak (Julian Glover) and Rena (Cyd Hayman) issue a terrible ultimatum to the personnel of Moonbase Alpha. (Alpha Child)

COLLISION COURSE

Screenplay **Anthony Terpiloff**
Directed by **Ray Austin**

The Moon is drawn on to a collision course with a massive planet – a collision which will almost certainly bring about the complete destruction of Moonbase Alpha. Victor comes up with a desperate plan to avert the disaster – speculating that the Moon could be diverted if a chain of nuclear mines are exploded in its path. As the preparations are made, a huge spaceship appears between the Moon and the planet and Koenig goes to investigate. Inside the ship he is greeted by an aged alien woman, Arra, who tells him that the people of her planet have awaited the Moon's arrival for millions of years and now, in order that a predetermined mutation can take place, the two astral bodies must be allowed to collide.

Guest Star

Arra	**Margaret Leighton**

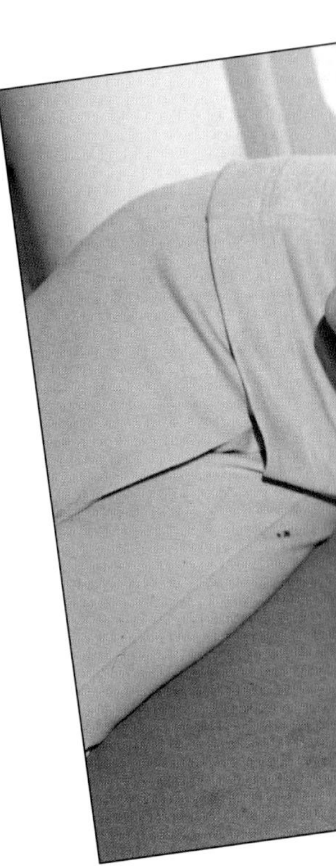

▲ Terribly injured, Koenig lies unconscious in a pool of his own blood. This graphic shot was cut from the final print of 'End of Eternity' and is shown here for the first time.

DEATH'S OTHER DOMINION

Screenplay **Anthony Terpiloff and Elizabeth Barrows**
Directed **Charles Crichton**

Koenig and a small landing party venture down onto the icy planet of Ultima Thule, following a radio transmission inviting them to share this lost paradise. The Alphans discover the survivors of the Uranus expedition of 1986 in subterranean caves, which had been lost in a proton storm. Dr Cabot Rowland explains that their ship had hit a time warp and they had been transported, not only through space, but also through time. They have all been on Ultima Thule for 880 years and none of them have aged a day! Now, believing themselves to be immortal, the explorers plan to rebuild their damaged ship, so that they may roam the universe for ever. Unfortunately for Dr Rowland, his extended lifespan comes with a high price, as he discovers when he tries to leave the planet.

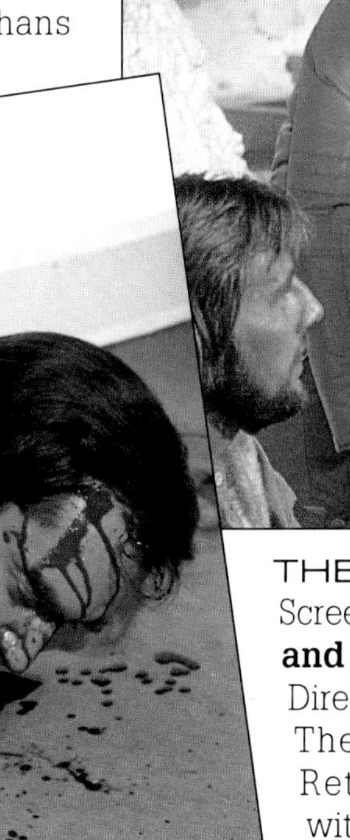

▲ On the icy planet of Ultima Thule, Bob Mathias (Anton Phillips) and Carter receive a warm welcome from its female inhabitants. (Death's Other Dominion)

Guest Stars

Dr Cabot Rowland	**Brian Blessed**
Captain Jack Tanner	**John Shrapnel**

THE FULL CIRCLE

Screenplay **Jesse Lasky Jr. and Pat Silver**
Directed by **Bob Kellett**

The mist-shrouded planet of Retha provides the Alphans with one of their most terrifying and inexplicable adventures. Investigating the disappearance of a survey team, Koenig and Helena venture into the strange mist and all contact with them is lost. Concerned for their safety, Carter sets out to find them, but is attacked by a group of primitive men and left for dead. Alone in the Eagle, Sandra is also attacked and taken to a nearby cave. As she witnesses the violent behaviour of the cave dwellers she gradually becomes aware that the leader of the tribe is none other than a bearded and fur-clad Commander Koenig!

END OF ETERNITY

Screenplay **Johnny Byrne**
Directed by **Ray Austin**

Blasting their way into a sealed asteroid, Koenig and a small team discover the body of a lone male occupant – unfortunately he has been critically injured by the explosion and Helena is doubtful that he will survive.

To everyone's amazement, the alien makes a full recovery and introduces himself as Balor, a scientist who had been imprisoned within the asteroid because he had achieved immortality for his people, thus removing all meaning from their lives. As events unfold, however, Balor is revealed as a dangerous psychopath who now intends to subject Alpha to a reign of terror.

Guest Stars

Balor	**Peter Bowles**
Mike Baxter	**Jim Smilie**

WAR GAMES

Screenplay **Christopher Penfold**
Directed by **Charles Crichton**

Moonbase Alpha is devastated when it comes under heavy attack from a squadron of Hawk fighters – highly advanced warships, originally from Earth! With half of Alpha's population dead and most of the Eagles wiped out, Koenig and Helena leave the wrecked base and travel to the enemy planet, in the hope of making peace with the unknown aggressor. In a futuristic city, the Alphans are confronted by a male and a female alien, who refuse their pleas for mercy, stating that the Alphans are no better than a virus and must not be allowed to destroy the Aliens perfect civilization. With no other choice open to him, Koenig returns to Alpha and prepares to launch an all-out attack.

Guest Stars

Male Alien	**Anthony Valentine**
Female Alien	**Isla Blair**

THE LAST ENEMY

Screenplay **Bob Kellett**
Directed by **Bob Kellett**

When the Moon drifts into a solar system in which two planets occupy an opposing orbit around their sun, Moonbase Alpha is caught in the middle of a war. Unable to fire directly at each other, the inhabitants of Betha and Delta are quick to see the potential of the Moon as a convenient gun platform and, within a very short space of time, a huge battlecruiser from Betha lands close to Alpha and launches a fusillade of missiles towards the other planet. Aware that the base is in very real danger, Koenig tries to negotiate a ceasefire between the two planets. For a while it looks as though he has succeeded, but he has reckoned without Dione, Betha's cunning and beautiful Chief Commissioner.

▲ As time runs out, Koenig travels to the enemy planet and tries to make peace with those who have sought to destroy them. (War Games)

Guest Stars

Dione	**Carolyn Mortimer**
Talos	**Kevin Stoney**

THE TROUBLED SPIRIT

Screenplay **Johnny Byrne**
Directed by **Ray Austin**

A hideously scarred figure stalks the corridors of Moonbase Alpha, bringing death to those it meets. As events unfold, Koenig

learns that botanist Dan Mateo has been conducting experiments in the hydroponics unit, experiments designed to prove that man is capable of using his telepathic powers to communicate with plants. Convinced that Mateo's experiments have conjured up some kind of psychic manifestation, Bergman holds a seance in the darkened surroundings of the botanist's lab. As Koenig and his colleagues join hands, the ghostly figure of another Dan Mateo materializes, this one terribly scarred, and demands atonement for his death – a death which has not yet occurred!

Guest Stars

Dan Mateo	**Giancarlo Prete**
Laura Adams	**Hilary Dwyer**
Dr James Warren	**Anthony Nicholls**
Spirit Mateo	**Val Musetti**

SPACE BRAIN

Screenplay **Christopher Penfold**
Directed by **Charles Crichton**

When mysterious alien hieroglyphics fill Alpha's video screens, an Eagle is sent out to investigate their apparent point of origin. As Koenig and his staff listen, the pilots report a pulsating space anemone, then all contact is lost. When a short while later a small meteorite strikes the Moon close to Alpha, Professor Bergman analyses it and discovers that it is the tightly compressed remains of the missing Eagle. Aware that Alpha faces certain destruction, Koenig orders an Eagle to be stocked with nuclear explosives and programmed to explode upon contact with the 'space brain'. The strange life form has other ideas, however, and by taking over the body of another Eagle pilot, it succeeds in communicating its true intentions.

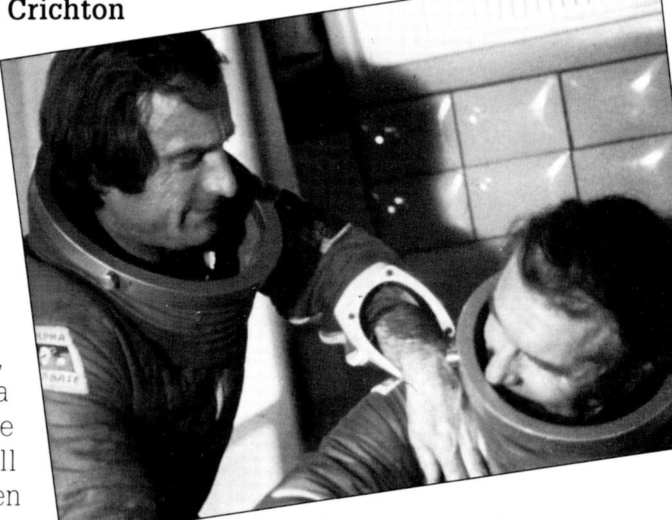

▲ In a sequence cut from the episode 'Space Brain', Alan Carter appears to wrestle with Kelly (Shane Rimmer), having just rescued him from the influence of the hypnotic space anemone.

Guest Stars

Kelly	**Shane Rimmer**
Melita Janni	**Carla Romanelli**

THE INFERNAL MACHINE

Screenplay **Anthony Terpiloff and Elizabeth Barrows**
Directed by **David Tomblin**

The personnel of Moonbase Alpha are amazed when a bizarre spaceship, one which really shouldn't be able to fly, approaches the Moon and a kindly but insistent voice asks for permission to land. At the invitation of the voice, Koenig, Helena and Victor enter the strange ship and meet an old man who identifies himself, quite simply, as Companion. He asks that the Alphans provide him with supplies for Gwent, which turns out to be the very ship itself – a living, thinking, feeling machine. When Companion dies, Gwent becomes disconsolate and informs his guests that they must now stay with him, his new Companions until the day they die.

Guest Star
Companion/Voice of Gwent **Leo McKern**

MISSION OF THE DARIANS

Screenplay **Johnny Byrne**
Directed by **Ray Austin**

When a colossal spaceship takes up a position above Alpha, Koenig and a small party respond to an urgent call for help. As they split up and explore, the Alphans encounter two separate colonies, clearly at odds with one another, existing in different sectors of the vast ship. Koenig and Victor encounter a civilized society, lead by the beautiful Kara, whilst the others encounter a group of savages – violent, primitive and intolerant of physical imperfection of any kind. As the secrets of the Darians are gradually revealed, Helena is imprisoned by the savages, who plan to sacrifice her to their god.

Guest Stars

Kara	**Joan Collins**
Petros	**Dennis Burgess**
Neman	**Aubrey Morris**
Hadin	**Robert Russell**

DRAGON'S DOMAIN

Screenplay **Christopher Penfold**
Directed by **Charles Crichton**

Astronaut Tony Cellini is a haunted man. Haunted not by any phantom spirit, but by memories – terrible memories of the ill-fated Ultra Probe expedition which, in 1996, had ended in disaster. According to Cellini, the probe ship, of which he was commander, had encountered an incredible collection of drifting, lifeless spacecraft. Lifeless except for the terrifying monster that had dwelt amongst the wrecks and had added his crew to its long list of victims. Cellini had barely escaped with his life, but no one except Koenig had ever believed his story, for it had seemed too ridiculous to be true – until now. When the self-same spaceships' graveyard appears on Alpha's screen, Cellini hijacks an Eagle and, with Koenig hot in pursuit, heads for a final showdown with his old enemy.

Guest Stars

Tony Cellini	**Gianni Garko**
Dr Monique Fauchere	**Barbara Kellerman**
Dr Darwin King	**Michael Sheard**
Prof Juliet Mackie	**Susan Jameson**

▼ The beautiful Kara (Joan Collins), welcomes the Alphans and invites them to join her on her galactic quest. But what is the terrible secret that lies at the heart of the Darian society?

◀ Guns at the ready, Koenig and Victor set out to explore the massive spaceship Daria, as it hovers above Alpha. (Mission of the Darians)

▼Having claimed the lives of the Ultra Probe crew, this horrific creature returns to menace Commander Koenig and the crew of Moonbase Alpha. (Dragon's Domain)

THE TESTAMENT OF ARKADIA

Screenplay **Johnny Byrne**
Directed by **David Tomblin**

The prospect of a slow, freezing death becomes a reality when, quite inexplicably, the Moon stops dead in space and Alpha's power starts to drain away. As time begins to run out, Koenig and a small landing party journey down to a bleak nearby planet where, in a small, dark cave, they discover an inscription in Sanskrit, the earliest written language known to man. As the inscription is translated, it is revealed that the human race originated there, on Arkadia, and that the coming of the Moon had been pre-ordained. For Koenig and the whole of Alpha it is an apocalyptic revelation, and for two Moonbase personnel in particular, it is the beginning of a brand new life.

Guest Stars

Luke Ferro	**Orso Maria Guerrini**
Anna Davis	**Liza Harrow**

◀ As security chief Tony Verdeschi, Tony Anholt was frequently given the chance to display the character's hot latin temperament.

Chapter 9

'Let's Do The Space Warp Again. . .'

In the autumn of 1975, *Space:1999* began its run on worldwide television and was met with a decidedly mixed response. In the UK the ever cautious programme planners ensured that, like *UFO*, it received fairly poor treatment on the ITV network, whilst in the US it was bought by a total of 155 PBS stations, 88 of these choosing to run it in a peak-time slot, in direct opposition to what was being broadcast by the three main networks. Gerry's disappointment at not achieving a network sale was tempered by the huge amount of American fan mail that his office received and, also, by ITC's decision to go ahead and commission a second series of 24 programmes.

Due to the overwhelming nature of the American response, it was firmly decided that the second series should be geared even more towards the US market and, with this in mind, Gerry Anderson recruited American Fred Freiberger to assume the role of producer, replacing Sylvia Anderson who had left the production for personal reasons. Freiberger, who had produced the third series of *Star Trek*, was greatly impressed by the programme's visual content, admitting that it was streets ahead of anything being made in America. He was however, highly critical of the cast and character development and instigated sweeping changes which would alter dramatically the style of the programme, leading to a few casualties along the way.

One of the first points made by Freiberger was to insist that more emphasis should be placed on relationships in an attempt to make the central characters appear more three-dimensional. As the new series began to take shape, so the tentative relationship which had previously existed between Koenig and Helena blossom into a fully fledged romance, a move which was clearly welcomed by both Martin Landau and Barbara Bain.

In order to create a more intimate environment in which to place the command team, the large but somehow bleak Main Mission set was ditched in favour of a much smaller underground control room known as Command Center (complete with American spelling!). Although an on-screen reason for the move was never given, it is widely accepted that, as a precaution against alien attack, Alpha's surface installations were abandoned and the entire crew relocated to the relative safety of the lower, subterranean levels.

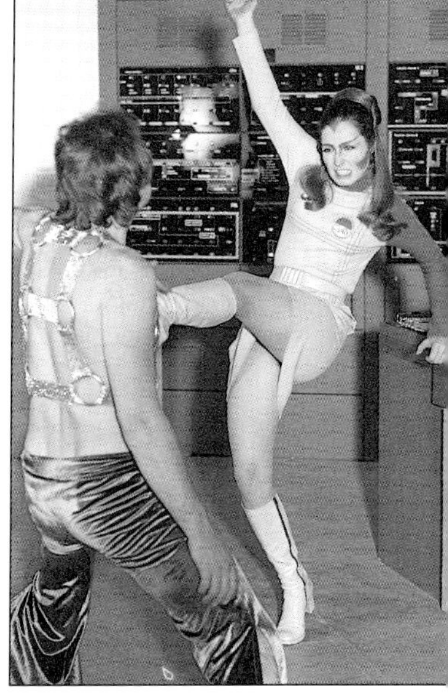

▲ As the Psycon beauty Maya, Catherine Schell high-kicked her way into the series and quickly established herself as one of the programme's most popular stars.

The most noticeable change made by Freiberger, however, was the inclusion of two dynamic new characters, brought in to replace Victor Bergman and Paul Morrow who, for various reasons, were left out of the new redeveloped plot.

Replacing Paul Morrow as Koenig's immediate second-in-command was Italian head of security Tony Verdeschi. Played by Tony Anholt (who had previously starred as Paul Buchet in *The Protectors*), Verdeschi was a likeable if rather quick-tempered young man who in his spare time liked

nothing more than to brew his own beer – much to the distaste of all those who tried it! Far more outrageous (and undeniably better looking!) was Maya – a fascinating alien shape-changer who, having encountered the Alphans on her home planet of Psychon, escapes with them when the planet explodes and joins the Moonbase personnel as science officer, a position formerly held by Professor Bergman. Played with great verve by the actress Catherine Schell (who had appeared in the previous season's 'Guardian of Piri'), Maya proved the point that not all aliens are unfriendly and together with Tony Verdeschi (with whom she soon developed a deep but playful relationship) she quickly became a popular and invaluable member of the team.

Filming commenced on 'The Metamorph', Johnny Byrne's opening story, on Monday 26 January, 1976; the script had originally been titled 'The Biological Soul' and had then undergone an extensive rewrite in order to introduce the character of Maya. Again, Brian Johnson was responsible for the quite stunning model effects, whilst the ever-dependable Charles Crichton, a man for whom Gerry Anderson has the greatest respect, was once more in the director's chair.

For personal reasons composer Barry Gray stepped down from the conductor's rostrum, and was replaced for the duration of the second season by former session musician and musical director of *Hair*, Derek Wadsworth. Having worked with Gerry Anderson on his semi-educational TV movie '*The Day After Tomorrow*', Wadsworth brought a lively, modern style of music to the series, which suited the revamped format better than the grandiose and largely orchestral pieces that Gray had composed for the previous season. Certainly Wadsworth's keyboard-oriented theme went well with the new, more 'immediate' opening title sequence and his guitar-laden incidental music added a certain momentum to the brisker, more action-packed episodes of the new series.

▲ Brian Johnson up-dated many of the models from the first series and, in this shot, a booster equipped Eagle is seen escaping from the doomed planet of Psychon.

▶ In the Grove of Psyche, Mentor (Brian Blessed) attends to his fantastic biological computer. (The Metamorph)

◀ As the second series took shape, so the relationship between Koenig and Doctor Russell was seen to blossom.

◀ Series two saw the demise of the huge Main Mission set and the introduction of the much smaller and far more intimate Command Center.

As with the previous season, the 24 new episodes consisted of a short 'hook', a much shorter epilogue and three 15 minute acts in between. The only significant difference was that the 'hook' now followed the opening titles and the epilogue was much lighter: the writers were encouraged to end each episode with a laugh, rather than the often profound conclusions which tended to round off most of the first season's stories.

This chapter covers all 24 episodes of the second season, which are, as before, presented in the actual order of production.

THE METAMORPH

Writer **Johnny Byrne**
Directed by **Charles Crichton**

On the planet Psychon, Koenig, Helena and Alan Carter discover a huge spaceship's graveyard and caves populated by mindless, zombie-like miners. Mentor, once the planet's greatest scientist, plans to revive the dead planet through the power of Psyche, an incredible biological computer of his own creation. Unfortunately, Psyche thrives upon stolen mental energy and the brain-dead cave dwellers are the pitiful results of Mentor's experimentation. With the population of Moonbase Alpha facing the same fate, Koenig manages to convince Maya, Mentor's daughter, of the truth behind her father's plan. Having been freed by the Psychon girl, the Alphans prepare to escape – but not before Koenig has smashed the computer and started a chain reaction which will destroy the planet.

Guest Stars

Mentor	**Brian Blessed**
Annette Fraser	**Anouska Hempel**
Ray Torens	**Nick Brimble**

THE EXILES

Writer **Donald James**
Directed by **Ray Austin**

When a fleet of small capsules approaches the Moon, one is brought down and, following an examination, it is discovered to contain the perfectly preserved body of a young man. The man revives and introduces himself as Cantar, telling the

Alphans that he and his people were exiled from their home planet, Golos, following a revolution. Agreeing to give Cantar and the rest of his people a home, Koenig sees to it that another capsule, this one containing Cantar's wife, Zova, is brought down and opened. Unfortunately, Cantar and Zova have ulterior motives and, using Alpha's power plant to generate a transporter beam, they travel across space to their home planet – taking Helena and Tony Verdeschi with them as hostages.

Guest Stars

Cantar	**Peter Duncan**
Zova	**Stacy Dorning**

ONE MOMENT OF HUMANITY

Writer **Tony Barwick**
Directed by **Charles Crichton**

Helena and Tony are transported to the planet Vega, where the apparently friendly Vegans offer them food and hospitality. Things are not as they seem, however, and it soon becomes apparent that the Vegans are not the generous hosts that at first they seemed. A robot-like servant, Number Eight, reveals himself to be a humanoid and informs the Alphans that the Vegans are the real robots, creations of a powerful computer, who intend to wipe out their servants as soon as they have provoked a violent reaction which they can copy. Determined not to rise to their bait, Helena and Tony find themselves suddenly back on a deserted Moonbase Alpha and it is not long before their own paranoia begins to get the better of them.

Guest Stars

Zamara	**Billie Whitelaw**
Zarl	**Leigh Lawson**
Number Eight	**Geoffrey Bayldon**

ALL THAT GLISTERS

Writer **Keith Miles**
Directed by **Ray Austin**

Koenig and a survey team venture down to a small planet in search of milgonite, a rare mineral essential to Alpha's life-support system. Geologist Dave O'Reilly is fascinated by a large glowing rock and lasers a piece off to test in the Eagle's laboratory. No sooner has the rock been returned to the ship than it reveals itself to be a strange life form and places Tony under hypnotic control. Attempting to find out what the rock wants, Maya transforms into a similar rock and tries to communicate with it. Unfortunately the alien rock begins to fuse with her and she seems unable to revert back to her natural form.

Guest Star

Dave O'Reilly	**Patrick Mower**

JOURNEY TO WHERE

Writer **Donald James**
Directed by **Tom Clegg**

When Moonbase Alpha receives a message from Texas City, Earth, it becomes apparent that, thanks to a revolutionary form of matter transporter, they will, at last, be able to return home. Koenig, Helena and Carter are the first to attempt the journey but, due to an earthquake in Texas, the trio are thrown off course and materialize in a damp and chilly area of unknown location. Unfortunately, due to Alpha's near-sterile environment, Helena quickly succumbs to

▼ Following an accident with a matter transporter, Koenig finds himself in 14th century Scotland, where he soon discovers that the locals are less than welcoming towards strangers. (Journey to Where)

pneumonia. The situation is made even worse when they are attacked and taken prisoner by a band of primitive warriors. As efforts are made to locate them, the wayward travellers make an incredible discovery – they have journeyed back in time to Scotland in the year 1339!

Guest Stars

Dr. Charles Logan	**Freddie Jones**
Carla	**Isla Blair**
MacDonald	**Roger Bizley**

THE TAYBOR

Writer **Thom Keyes**
Directed by **Bob Brooks**

Taybor, an intergalactic trader, materializes on the Moon; bringing with him a horde of exotic and beautiful treasures and the possibility of a return to Earth. Taybor's ship, the SS Emporium, is equipped with a remarkable jump-drive, which allows him to enter hyperspace and traverse the universe with ease. Realizing the potential of such a system, Koenig offers Taybor the very Moon in return for the system's plans. Taybor isn't keen on Koenig's offer, but does have something in mind for which he would be prepared to trade – Maya! Naturally Koenig refuses to agree but, seeing that Taybor is clearly besotted with the Psychon girl, he suggests an altogether more acceptable alternative.

Guest Star

Taybor	**Willoughby Goddard**

▲ When an intergalactic trader (Willoughby Goddard) arrives on Alpha, the personnel greet him with open arms, only to discover that he demands a high price in return for his goods.

THE MARK OF ARCHANON

Writer **Lee Scwartz**
Directed by **Charles Crichton**

In a deep lunar cavern, Alan Carter discovers two alien bodies – a boy and a man – both perfectly preserved in a glass chamber. Freeing them, he is amazed to discover that they are still alive! When they have recovered, the adult introduces himself as Pasc and the boy as his son, Etrec. As Helena and Tony listen, Pasc explains that he had been the leader of an ancient expedition to Earth and had been overpowered by those of his own people who had been infected by the very evil which infested the planet. As events unfold, however, it is discovered that both Pasc and Etrec carry a genetic sickness which will soon turn them both in psychopathic killers!

Guest Stars

Pasc	**John Standing**
Etrec	**Michael Gallagher**

◀ **Far Left:** On an otherwise barren world, Alan, Koenig and geologist Dave O'Reilly (Patrick Mower) discover a huge crystal formation which appears to consist of badly needed Milgonite. (All that Glisters)

THE RULES OF LUTON

Writer **Charles Woodgrove**
Directed by **Val Guest**

Whilst exploring a lush, Earth-like planet, Koenig eats some wild berries and Maya picks a beautiful flower. A terrible scream echoes around the glade and a powerful voice informs them that they must be punished for their murderous acts. On Luton, which they learn is the name of the planet, plants are the dominant life form – indeed, the Judges of Luton, who address them via Koenig's commlock screen, appear to be a triad of talking trees. Unwilling to listen to their pleas, the Judges sentence the Alphans to trial by combat with three other alien criminals. With their weapons out of action and unable to communicate with Alpha, Koenig and Maya must fight for survival against three unusually gifted opponents.

Guest Stars

Alien Strong	**David Jackson**
Alien Invisible	**Roy Marsden**
Alien Transport	**Godfrey James**

BRIAN THE BRAIN

Writer **Jack Ronder**
Directed by **Kevin Connor**

Approaching a small, apparently unremarkable planet, the personnel of Moonbase Alpha are surprised when a Swift spaceship from Earth comes into view and lands on the base. The ship is uninhabited, except for a cheeky talking computer named Brian. Brian explains that the Swift had been launched to explore the nearby planet – simply known as Planet D – in 1996. Unfortunately, the entire crew had died on the planet's surface and he has been in orbit ever since. Inviting Helena and Koenig aboard his ship, Brian abducts them and takes off, heading for Planet D, where his true intentions are soon made clear.

Guest Star

Brian/Captain Michael	**Bernard Cribbins**

NEW ADAM, NEW EVE

Writer **Terence Feely**
Directed by **Charles Crichton**

An imposing, sage-like figure materializes in Alpha's Command Center and announces that he is Magus – the creator of all life on Earth. He tells the enthralled assembly that he is prepared to give the Alphans that which he has never given any other race in

▲ In what appears to be a veritable Garden of Eden, a figure claiming to be God (Guy Rolfe) offers Koenig and his colleagues the chance to start again. (New Adam, New Eve)

▲ **Above left:** On the planet of Luton, Koenig fights for his life against a supremely powerful opponent. (The Rules of Luton)

the cosmos – the chance to begin again in a new Eden. Koenig, Helena, Tony and Maya are chosen to be the new Adams and new Eves, and are transported by Magus to a lush nearby planet. However, like the Eden of old, the new Eden contains its own serpent and it is not long before the Alphans discover the truth about Magus and the secret behind his elaborate façade.

Guest Stars

Magus	**Guy Rolfe**
Humanoid	**Bernard Kay**

THE A B CHRYSALIS

Writer **Tony Barwick**
Directed by **Val Guest**

Massive shockwaves, hitting Alpha at regular intervals, threaten to destroy the base as it approaches their point of origin. Discovering that the shockwaves are coming from a distant planet, Koenig, Alan and Maya set out in an Eagle to try and put a stop to the dangerous bombardment. Beneath the surface of the planet, the Alphans encounter sphere-like probes and learn that these probes are indeed creating the shockwaves in an attempt to destroy the approaching Moon, which they see as a threat to their creators, the Masters, who, upon death, enter a vulnerable chrysalis stage before being reborn. As time begins to run out, Koenig must convince two newly reborn Masters that the Moon poses no threat and must be allowed to continue its voyage in peace.

Guest Stars

Chrysalis A	**Ina Skriver**
Chrysalis B	**Sarah Douglas**

▼ Koenig encounters powerful resistance when he tries to enter the underground lair of the sleeping Masters. (The A B Chrysalis)

CATACOMBS OF THE MOON

Writer **Anthony Terpiloff**
Directed by **Robert Lynn**

Michelle Osgood lies ill in the medical centre: only an artificial heart can save her life. In the catacombs beneath the Moon, Patrick, Michelle's husband, is caught in an explosion and has visions of Alpha being consumed by a raging fire. Hallucination or premonition? When a freak heatwave hits the base, Koenig takes off in an Eagle to investigate and discovers a tremendous firestorm heading directly for Alpha. Meanwhile, Tony and Helena have more immediate problems as Osgood snatches his wife from the medical centre and flees into the darkened tunnels.

Guest Stars

Patrick Osgood	**James Laurenson**
Michelle Osgood	**Pamela Stephenson**

SEED OF DESTRUCTION

Writer **John Goldsmith**
Directed by **Kevin Connor**

When a mysterious power loss endangers Moonbase Alpha, Koenig and Alan travel to a jewel-like asteroid which appears to be the source of the problem. Exploring a fantastic crystal cave, resembling a vast hall of mirrors, Koenig is unprepared for an attack from an unexpected source, when his reflection takes on a life of its own and strikes him down. Leaving the real Koenig imprisoned within the crystal matrix, the doppelgänger Koenig returns to Alpha and immediately arranges for a powerful energy beam to be projected at the asteroid. Meanwhile the real Commander Koenig learns that the asteroid is, in fact, a complex living organism which needs Alpha's power in order to regenerate itself.

THE BETA CLOUD

Writer **Charles Woodgrove**
Directed by **Robert Lynn**

When a strange cloud appears in the Moon's path, almost everyone on Alpha, including Commander Koenig, is afflicted with a debilitating fever. As Tony Verdeschi takes command, a terrifying creature bursts into Alpha and, meeting with very little resistance, rampages through the base causing havoc on a massive scale. A voice from the cloud announces that the creature has been sent to take the power core from Alpha's life support system, which it needs to prevent itself from becoming extinct. With the lives of everyone at stake, Tony and Maya must find a way of stopping the relentless intruder, before it can reach its destination.

Guest Star

Beta Cloud Creature	**Dave Prowse**

A MATTER OF BALANCE

Writers **Pip and Jane Baker**
Directed by **Charles Crichton**

Botanist Shermeen Williams is visited by the spirit-body of an alien calling himself Vindrus. The alien explains that his world is a world of antimatter and that it is heading for extinction. The only hope for he and his people is if they can cross over into the universe of matter. A temple-like building on a beautiful planet contains the apparatus necessary for such a transition – a matter/antimatter converter. Agreeing to help Vindrus, Shermeen steals a portable generator and activates the machine. Unfortunately there is a catch: to maintain the equilibrium, every antimatter being who crosses over must be replaced by someone from the matter universe – and that means someone from Moonbase Alpha!

Guest Stars

Shermeen Williams	**Lynne Frederick**
Vindrus	**Stuart Wilson**

▼ On an Earth-like planet, botanist Shermeen Williams succumbs to the influence of Vindrus, a scheming anti-matter being. A publicity shot of Lynne Fredrick and Stuart Wilson, taken on location for 'A Matter of Balance'

SPACE WARP

Writer **Charles Woodgrove**
Directed by **Peter Medak**

Koenig and Tony are investigating a derelict spaceship when the Moon falls through a space warp, transporting it five light years from its previous position. Marooned on the alien vessel, Koenig and Tony discover a recorded log which may help them to locate the position of the now invisible space warp. Meanwhile, as the personnel of Moonbase Alpha come to terms with their new situation, a far more immediate problem arises. Maya, who has been struck down by a mystery illness, becomes delirious and, transforming into an alien creature, rampages through Alpha, leaving a trail of destruction in her wake.

Guest Star

Petrov	**Peter Porteous**

THE BRINGERS OF WONDER - Part One

Writer **Terence Feely**
Directed by **Tom Clegg**

Following a serious accident, Koenig lies unconscious in the medical centre, his mind attached to a new cerebral-wave machine designed to counteract the potentially damaging affects of concussion. While he is unconscious, what appears to be a faster-than-light Superswift spaceship lands on the Moon – the crew seemingly intent on rescuing the Alphans and taking them back to Earth. Carter and two radiation experts become the envy of everyone when they are chosen to be the first to make the long voyage home. No sooner have they taken off than Koenig recovers and makes his way to Command Center – nothing can prepare him for the sight which greets him. Instead of long-lost friends, he sees Alpha's visitors as hideous one-eyed monsters!

THE BRINGERS OF WONDER - Part Two

Writer **Terence Feely**
Directed by **Tom Clegg**

Having survived one attempt on his life, Koenig realizes that the cerebral wave machine must have prevented him from succumbing to the aliens' hypnotic powers. With difficulty he persuades Maya to undergo the same treatment and, with her mind clear, she is able to confirm Koenig's story. It is soon discovered that the aliens plan to blow up the Moon's remaining nuclear waste dumps so that they can absorb the radiation generated during the explosion. Believing that they are now on Earth, Alan, Ehlrich and Bartlett begin the process which will trigger the massive explosion. As time begins to run out, only Commander Koenig can save the personnel of Moonbase Alpha from complete and utter annihilation.

Guest Stars

Guido Verdeschi	**Stuart Damon**
Diana Morris	**Toby Robins**
Jack Bartlett	**Jeremy Young**
Joe Ehlrich	**Drewe Henley**
Professor Hunter	**Billy J. Mitchell**
Dr Shaw	**Patrick Westwood**

▲ Terror in Command Center as Alpha's unexpected guests are revealed for what they really are! (Bringers of Wonder)

THE LAMBDA FACTOR
Writer **Terrance Dicks**
Directed by **Charles Crichton**

A series of unexplained disturbances affects the smooth running of Moonbase Alpha: Koenig is haunted by ghosts from his past and increased paranormal activity is monitored in a number of personnel. Eventually, a mysterious space-cloud is identified as the source of the trouble and Maya explains that it is giving off lamda waves, a form of energy which amplifies natural psychic ability. One Alphan in particular, Carolyn Powell, seems to possess greater powers than most and, having taken control of the Command Center, enters into a battle of minds with Commander Koenig – a battle from which only one of them can emerge.

Guest Stars

Carolyn Powell	**Deborah Fallender**
Mark Sanders	**Jess Conrad**
Carl Renton	**Michael Walker**
Peter Garforth	**Gregory de Polnay**

THE SEANCE SPECTRE
Writer **Donald James**
Directed by **Peter Medak**

Greg Sanderson and his surface exploration team are furious when they are denied access to Command Center – especially since the Moon is now approaching a freak weather belt which may contain a habitable planet. Using stun-guns to knock out the Command personnel, Sanderson and his colleagues hold a seance and announce that the weather belt does indeed contain a planet which could sustain them. Koenig and Maya, meanwhile, have ventured into the weather belt in an Eagle and located a planet in its midst. The planet turns out to be nothing more than a barren and inhospitable rock – a lifeless world which, to make matters worse, is on a collision course with the Moon!

Greg Sanderson	**Ken Hutchison**
Cernik	**Nigel Pegram**
Eva	**Carolyn Seymour**
Stevens	**James Snell**

DORZAK
Writer **Christopher Penfold**
Directed by **Val Guest**

Following an urgent request for assistance, a spaceship from the planet Norvah is allowed to land on Alpha. The occupants of the ship turn out to be two beautiful women, Sahala and Yesta and their prisoner, a Psychon named Dorzak. Sahala explains that Dorzak had arrived on their planet, fleeing from his own world which he knew was nearing destruction, and had incited her people to violence after thousands of years of peace. They are now taking him to a place of exile, the planet Thesalena. Maya is unconvinced by the story, remembering Dorzak as a peaceful philosopher, and insists upon releasing him from stasis. Unfortunately, Dorzak is revealed to be a changed man and a dangerous one at that!

Guest Stars

Dorzak	**Lee Montague**
Sahala	**Jill Townsend**
Yesta	**Kathryn Leigh Scott**
Clea	**Seretta Wilson**

DEVIL'S PLANET
Writer **Michael Winder**
Directed by **Tom Clegg**

In response to a distress signal, Koenig journeys to a nearby planet, only to find a transporter booth surrounded by dead bodies. It quickly becomes apparent that the air contains a dangerous pathogen to which the Alphans are immune, but which has proven deadly to the other arrivals. In order to solve the mystery, Koenig lands on the planet's moon, only to be taken prisoner by a band of scarlet-clad, whip-bearing women. Koenig soon discovers that he is on a penal colony and that Elizia, the colony's overseer, is allowing prisoners to transport down to the planet's surface as a reward for good behaviour, secretly aware that they will die upon contact with the atmosphere. Determined to prevent further injustice, Koenig enters a transporter booth and challenges Elizia to follow.

▶ Archon (Patrick Troughton), the Dorcon ruler whose quest for immortality can only be achieved upon the death of Maya.

▶ **Far right:** In a sealed structure, Koenig and his survey team discover the wizened body of a long-dead explorer. (The Immunity Syndrome)

▼ Beautiful but cruel. These whip-wielding women ensure that the inmates of Entra's penal colony are kept well under control. (Devil's Planet)

Guest Stars

Elizia	**Hildgarde Neil**
Crael	**Roy Marsden**

THE IMMUNITY SYNDROME

Writer **Johnny Byrne**
Directed by **Bob Brooks**

An expedition to an Earth-like planet turns into a nightmare when, for no apparent reason, Tony Verdeschi seems to go mad, killing another member of the team and disappearing into a forest. The situation worsens as an inexplicable change in the atmosphere causes rapid corrosion of all their metal equipment – effectively stranding them and cutting off all communication with Alpha. In a sealed chamber, Koenig and Alan discover the wizened corpse of a long-dead explorer and, by replaying a prerecorded message, they learn that the planet is inhabited by an immortal light-being, the sight of which is enough to cause insanity. In order to save the lives of his colleagues, Koenig realizes that he must locate the being and find a safe way of communicating with it.

Guest Stars

Zoran	**Nadim Sawalha**
The Voice	**Hal Galili**

THE DORCONS

Writer **Johnny Byrne**
Directed by **Tom Clegg**

Maya is abducted from Alpha by a Dorcon energy beam and transported to their hovering space ship. In a desperate attempt to save her, Koenig throws himself into the beam and is similarly transported away. On the Dorcon ship it soon becomes clear that Maya's brain stem is to be removed and transplanted into Archon, an aged Dorcon leader. The operation will mean death for Maya, but immortality for Archon. Koenig succeeds in rescuing Maya but before they can escape they become embroiled in a plot by Malic, Archon's heir, to kill his father and claim both the throne and immortality for himself.

Guest Stars

Archon	**Patrick Troughton**
Consul Varda	**Ann Firbank**
Malic	**Gerry Sundquist**

▲ Tony Arnholt has little chance but to submit to inspection by an inquisitive simian guest star.

Chapter 10

The Lion in Winter
and other near misses

'There's nothing quite like stepping out of your office and coming face to face with a fully-grown lion to get your day off to a bad start, I can tell you!' Gerry Anderson smiles as he recounts one of the many incidents which caused him a headache or two during the making of *Space:1999*. It seems funny now, but at the time, the inclusion of wild animals into the second season's format could have ended in disaster.

With complete control over her molecular structure, Maya had the ability to transform herself into any living creature in the blink of an eye. As well as insects, birds and field mice, the Psychon would, during the course of the series, wear the forms of, amongst other things, a wolf, a tiger, a panther and the aforementioned lion. Despite assurances from its handler, who had let the beast roam free during a tea-break, a hasty phone call to circus owner Billy Smart confirmed that there was no such thing as a tame big cat and, from that moment on, Mr Smart and his company were hired to provide and supervise every wild animal that the production required.

Creatures of a far more bizarre nature would also appear frequently throughout the new series, as the Alphans began to encounter terrible and hostile monsters, of the variety usually found only in the BBC's *Doctor Who*. Following the undoubted success of the octopod creature from 'Dragon's Domain', monster stories quickly became the backbone of the show and it seemed that every new planet or gloomily-lit corridor concealed a rubber-suited horror, just waiting to pounce. One creature in particular, a bug-eyed reptilian giant, would appear in no less than three episodes, suitably patched up and redressed on each occasion!

Eager that the second series should not take as long to complete as the first, which had been almost 18 months in the making, the production team used every trick in the book in order to speed up the process without losing any of the existing high standards along the way. One such ploy, and possibly the most effective, was to film two episodes at the same time, utilizing separate sound stages at Pinewood and locations within Black Park in nearby

◀ During its second year, Space:1999 featured an assortment of weird and wonderful alien monsters. Here, actor Albin Pahernik is made ready on the set of 'The A B Chrysalis'.

Iver Heath. Altogether eight episodes were shot in this way and, of these, Martin Landau is absent from 'Dorzak', whilst Barbara Bain is seen only briefly in 'Devil's Planet' and then only by virtue of footage re-used from earlier episodes. Another point worth noting here is that both Landau and Bain were absent from the episode 'The Beta Cloud', as they were on holiday abroad while it was being filmed. Landau's role in the episode, which was to have been a significant one, was taken instead by Tony Anholt.

In December 1976, as filming was completed on 'The Dorcons', production of *Space:1999* finally drew to a close. By then, the British viewing public had already been introduced to the series, 'The Metamorph' having premiered on ATV on Saturday 4th September, but with regional screenings just as sporadic as they had been the previous year, the chances of a third series being commissioned must have seemed unlikely to say the least. In America, where the series had enjoyed such an enthusiastic welcome, the story was a very similar one. Again, quite inexplicably, the networks passed it by in favour of less advanced home-grown fare and, as it began to go out around the country in syndication, it quickly became apparent that the show was being received less warmly the second time around. True, a fair number of dedicated fans continued to follow the show every week but, without the significant audience it had attracted before, the programme was a ratings loser and, long before the 24 new episodes had completed their stateside run, it became painfully clear that there would be no more. If, in the final analysis, *Space:1999* must be seen to have missed its large projected audience, then by contrast, it must also be regarded as an artistic and creative success. Never before or

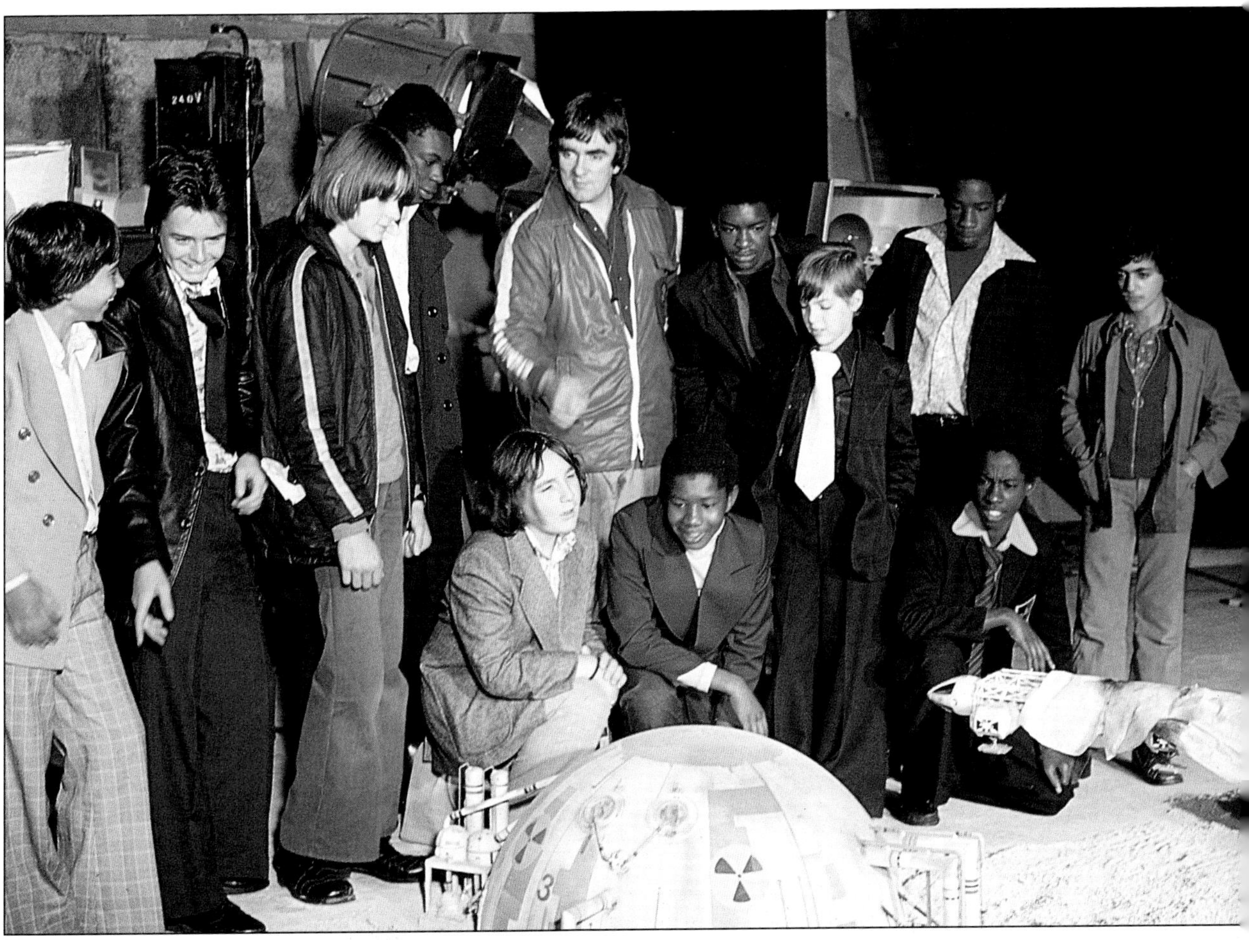

▲ In the props store at Pinewood, the show's principal cast enjoy a good laugh with some of their less attractive guest stars.

◀ **Above right:** At the special effects studio in Bray, Brian Johnson shows some young fans one of his highly detailed miniature sets.

◀ An extremely unusual publicity shot of Barbara Bain, repelling the advances of an unknown assailant.

since has a series so perfectly captured the sense of wonder and excitement that will surely be felt by Earth's future pioneers when they do eventually journey out into the mysterious regions of uncharted space. Visually, the series was stunning and, even with today's advanced computer-assisted techniques, it is difficult to see how some of the better model shots could be improved upon. In short, *Space:1999* has stood the test of time remarkably well and, viewed with even the most critical eye, the better episodes of the series look as fresh today as they must have done all those years ago.

Today, 20 years since it was first committed to film, the series is finding a whole new audience, thanks to its release on sell-through video and currently enjoys great popularity amongst an ever-growing legion of hardcore enthusiasts. According to Chris Bentley, chairman of Fanderson (the official Gerry Anderson Appreciation Society), interest in the series is very much on the increase at the moment and, along with *UFO*, *Captain Scarlet* and *Thunderbirds*, it is widely regarded as Anderson's most accomplished and popular show. Certainly it has been the subject of a specially produced video documentary and, along with *UFO*'s 'Sub-Smash', 'Breakaway' is the episode most frequently requested for screening at the society's regular and well-attended conventions.

A life-long fan of Anderson's work, Bentley has a particular fondness for the live-action series and describes *UFO* and *Space:1999* as 'two of the finest science-fiction television series ever produced.' As *Stingray*, *Thunderbirds* and *Captain Scarlet* enjoy renewed success thanks to high-profile BBC reruns, it is surely only a matter of time before *UFO* and *Space:1999* are picked up by a responsible broadcaster and, for the first time, receive the recognition that they have been denied for so long.

▲ The Eagle leaves its pad, perhaps for the last time.

Epilogue

A heavy silence hung over Main Mission like a cloak. The banks of computers which had once chattered and blinked as they processed a never ending stream of information, stood silent, their electronic minds as dead as the base itself. Without its desks, chairs and human inhabitants, the nerve centre of Moonbase Alpha was nothing more than a cave – a huge, bleak, geometrically perfect cave. An empty hole at the centre of an equally empty web.

'All right Professor, you've got three minutes.' Snapped out of his reverie by the sound of the voice, Victor Bergman looked round and saw Paul, good old dependable Paul, standing with his finger on the record button of the electronic Alpha log – the only piece of operational equipment destined to remain on the base. A base which, in five minutes' time, they would leave behind for ever.

As he cleared his throat, his mind searching for the words he had never expected to say, Victor glanced across at the silent figures who watched him closely from the other side of the room, the pale starlight bathing their features in a thin, spectral glow. Kano, his dark, impassive face showing the strain of the last few hours and Sandra, so young, so frightened, her eyes reflecting the fear that he knew they all felt. How long had he known them. . .how much had they been through together. . .how could they leave the base now, unsure as they were of what lay ahead?

At last the Professor spoke, his voice, normally so confident, so certain, wavered as if at the enormity of what he knew he was about to say.

'We are mankind,' he began, pausing as if to add importance to his simple opening line. 'We came from planet Earth and we built this base, called Alpha, to learn more about the universe in which we live. Unfortunately, due to human error, this moon was blasted out of Earth's orbit and we have for the last year, travelled through space; wanderers in search of a new place to call home.' He paused, looking round at the small group which huddled by the window. Paul had joined Sandra now and had placed a strong protective arm around her. Victor smiled to himself. Paul would look after her, he would see that she was all right. 'Now we can no longer live here,' he continued, 'and we go to face an uncertain future on the planet which has nearly destroyed us.' Again he paused, swallowing hard as he remembered the lives that had been lost; the personnel, the colleagues, the friends who had been snuffed out like candles as the base had rocked beneath the enemy's attack. 'You, whoever you are, who find this empty vessel of Alpha, come and seek us out, if we still exist – come and teach us all you know, because, if we have learned anything during our journey, we have learned that we still have much to learn.' Nodding to his companions, and knowing that there was nothing more to say, Victor switched off the machine and walked, very slowly, towards the main door. On the threshold, he turned back and looked, for one last time, at the place he had grown to think of as home. 'Goodbye Alpha,' he said, so quietly that the others couldn't hear him then, without another glance, he turned on his heel and made his way towards the waiting Eagle and the uncertain future which he knew lay ahead.

◀ 'Goodbye Alpha. . .